THE ETHICS OF GIVING

THE ETHICS OF GIVING

Philosophers' Perspectives on Philanthropy

Edited by Paul Woodruff

OXFORD
UNIVERSITY PRESS

OXFORD
UNIVERSITY PRESS

Oxford University Press is a department of the University of Oxford. It furthers
the University's objective of excellence in research, scholarship, and education
by publishing worldwide. Oxford is a registered trade mark of Oxford University
Press in the UK and certain other countries.

Published in the United States of America by Oxford University Press
198 Madison Avenue, New York, NY 10016, United States of America.

Library of Congress Cataloging-in-Publication Data
Names: Woodruff, Paul, 1943– editor.
Title: The ethics of giving : philosophers' perspectives on philanthropy /
[edited by] Paul Woodruff.
Description: New York : Oxford University Press, 2018. |
Includes bibliographical references and index.
Identifiers: LCCN 2017041322 | ISBN 9780190648879 (hardback) |
ISBN 9780190648893 (epub)
Subjects: LCSH: Charities—Philosophy. | Humanitarianism—Philosophy.
Classification: LCC HV25 .E85 2018 | DDC 174/.43617—dc23
LC record available at https://lccn.loc.gov/2017041322

1 3 5 7 9 8 6 4 2

Printed by Sheridan Books, Inc., United States of America

CONTENTS

ACKNOWLEDGMENTS

These papers were written for this volume; most of them were presented at a conference convened by John Deigh, Jonathan Dancy, and Paul Woodruff. The conference was supported by the Royal Professorship in Ethics and American Society and also by the Once Upon a Time Foundation, which is devoted to promoting discussion about philanthropy. We are all grateful to Geoffrey Raynor, who founded a program of university courses called The Philanthropy Lab, which gave rise to the discussions that led to this project, and who also funds the Once Upon a Time Foundation.

I am grateful to John Deigh and Jonathan Dancy for advice and editorial suggestions. Anonymous readers for Oxford University Press have been helpful as well. My largest debt is to my assistant editor, J. Drake, who helped with format and judgments about content.

LIST OF CONTRIBUTORS

Elizabeth Ashford is a senior lecturer in philosophy at the University of St. Andrews. She works in moral and political philosophy and is currently completing a book, *Hunger's Unwitting Executioners: Severe Poverty as a Structural Human Rights Violation*, under contract with Oxford University Press.

Brandon Boesch is a PhD candidate in philosophy at the University of South Carolina. Aside from work in applied ethics, he has also published articles on the topic of representation in science.

Thomas E. Hill Jr. is Kenan professor at the University of North Carolina at Chapel Hill. He is the author of *Virtue, Rules, and Justice: Kantian Aspirations* (Oxford University Press, 2012) and *Human Welfare and Moral Worth: Kantian Perspectives* (Oxford University Press, 2002) and the editor of *A Blackwell Guide to Kant's Ethics* (Wiley-Blackwell, 2009).

William MacAskill is an associate professor of philosophy at the University of Oxford. He is the author of *Doing Good Better* (Penguin Random House, 2015).

Jeff McMahan is White's Professor of Moral Philosophy at the University of Oxford. He is the author of *The Ethics of Killing: Problems at the Margins of Life* (Oxford University Press, 2002) and *Killing in War* (Oxford University Press, 2009).

Andreas Mogensen is a tutorial fellow at Jesus College and an associate professor of philosophy at Oxford University. He has published articles on moral epistemology, especially on evolutionary debunking arguments.

Toby Ord is a research fellow at the Future of Humanity Institute at Oxford University. He has published on topics including global poverty and moral uncertainty.

Christine Swanton is at the Philosophy Department of the University of Auckland. She is the author of *The Virtue Ethics of Hume and Nietzsche* (Wiley Blackwell, 2015) and *Virtue Ethics: A Pluralistic View* (Oxford University Press, 2003). Recent and forthcoming work include papers on virtue ethics and role ethics, and virtue ethics and particularism.

Paul Woodruff is Darrel K. Royal Professor of Ethics and American Society at the University of Texas at Austin. He is the author of *Reverence: Renewing a Forgotten Virtue* (2d edition, Oxford University Press, 2014) and *The Ajax Dilemma: Justice and Fairness in Rewards* (Oxford University Press, 2011).

THE ETHICS OF GIVING

Introduction

PAUL WOODRUFF

Philanthropy can be a matter of life and death, for both people and institutions. Some human lives depend on philanthropy, and so does the quality of life for many others. Philanthropy is especially impor- tant to us who teach at institutions supported by donations; we de- pend on those who raise money to support, among other things, philosophy. Yet few of us have dealt directly with hard questions about the subject.

Philosophy matters more for philanthropy than for most subjects in ethics, because differences in theory point to different philan- thropic practices. Consequentialism, for example, calls us to give where our giving can do the most good, generally in terms of lives saved or health restored; for us in the first world, this means giving to people who are far away from us. Virtue ethics, if situated in social practices, may call for a more localized approach to giving. And if justice requires the wealthy to return wealth to those who should, in justice, have had it in the first place (as Kant suggests), then justice asks the wealthy to determine who are the rightful owners of their wealth. Justice may also require us to guarantee human rights, in- cluding the rights that are violated by systemic poverty.

In editing this volume, we have been looking for a variety of theoretical approaches to ethics that answer such questions as these:

Why should one give? What is it that wealthy tightwads do not understand? Is generosity a virtue? Do we have duties to give? If we do, then clearly we will be in the wrong if we do not give. And a question follows: Are philanthropic duties narrow or wide? If narrow, these duties would be specific to particular causes and perhaps would require us to give specified amounts. How are the causes and amounts to be determined? But perhaps philanthropy is supererogatory—a good deed beyond the call of duty, earning merit when done, but not blame when left undone. What is the connection between philanthropy and altruism: can one be a selfish or self-interested philanthropist? How should philanthropists weigh the values of various causes, such as religion, the arts, education, human rights, animal rights, and saving lives from hunger or disease? Is it wrong to give money to the arts when that money could have saved lives?

This volume contains essays by prominent philosophers, most of whom are new to the subject. Our aim has been to attract new minds and voices to a philosophical discussion of philanthropy. Virtue ethics and Kantian ethics are represented here, in addition to more familiar consequentialist approaches.

On philanthropy, more than on most other subjects in ethics, recent philosophers have theories that diverge widely from common practices. Most people who are thought to be living ethical lives seem to give very little to philanthropic causes, and what they do give is rarely as effective as it could be. Few people do the most good they can by way of philanthropy. Yet most of us share the intuition that we should save a drowning child if we come across one and can do so with little risk or loss to ourselves, and we agree that a passerby would do wrong to leave the child to drown. But distance makes these intuitions fade. If we hear news of a child drowning on the other side of the world, would we do wrong not to pull out our checkbooks?

Charitable giving in fact often shows a bias toward the local. Is partiality of this kind irrational? Does it represent a moral failure? If so, it is a very widespread failure. Another challenge: local giving often shows a bias toward religion, education, and the arts; admirable though these causes may be, they do little to alleviate human suffering compared with causes that save children from starvation or the ravages of malaria.

Most moral theories explain common moral intuitions to some extent. Kant assumes that his readers agree about such issues as false promising and then shows how his theory can provide grounds for such agreement. In the case of philanthropy, some recent philosophers have taken a different role. Instead of grounding principles that lie behind what is generally considered ethical giving, they have argued for a kind of giving that is different from the norm, to which the name "effective altruism" has been given. Effective altruism calls for contributions to causes that can be shown, quantitatively, to do the most good. Its prime advocate is Peter Singer; Will MacAskill, whose work appears in this volume, has also written eloquently in its favor.

One need not be a consequentialist to advocate effective altruism, although the principal spokespeople for the movement have been consequentialists. Elizabeth Ashford, also in this volume, has offered a justice-based argument that supports effective altruism. Kantians and virtue ethicists could come to similar conclusions. But theories differ over whether it is wrong to choose a lesser good: If I can do the most good by donating to Oxfam, but I choose instead to effect a lesser good by giving to the local library, have I done wrong? Strong act utilitarians will be inclined to say that I have, but ethicists from other schools of thought will not agree. Jeff McMahan in this volume shows that, when it is not wrong to give nothing, it does not appear to be wrong to give toward a lesser good. Thomas Hill shows why a Kantian would approve of gifts to the arts and education, and Brandon Boesch argues for a concept of integrity that competes with utilitarian considerations. Christine Swanton's theory of virtue opens new, nonutilitarian ways of thinking about such matters. I have added my own thoughts on justice as an afterword.

Here I offer brief summaries of the chapters.

1. Thomas E. Hill Jr., "Duties and Choices in Philanthropic Giving: Kantian Perspectives." Philosophers before Hill have done little to explore the implications of Kant's theory for philanthropy. Hill has a distinguished record as an interpreter of Kant and also as a philosopher who, in his own right, applies Kantian method to ethical issues not directly addressed by Kant. The principal method is that of systematic moral legislation on a rational basis. Applying this to the human situation, Kantians propose principles that aspire to be worthy of agreement by reason-governed human beings.

Philanthropy fulfills a duty that is wide or imperfect, in Kant's vocabulary—meaning that it is not specific about how, when, and how much to help others. But it falls under a strict duty to make the happiness of others an end of our own. That is, moral law requires us to be philanthropic but leaves us some latitude as to how to do this. It does not require us to be impartial with regard to family, friends, or neighbors. The principle of beneficence as Hill understands it is not a decision procedure for all cases and does not determine in every case an action one should take. It is, after all, one principle in a system of moral legislation; other principles, which may be more demanding, will probably apply to a case in question. For example, a principle of mutual aid (such as that of Rawls) is essentially Kantian and is more determinate than the duty of beneficence.

In responding to objections Hill explains why Kant prescribes a duty to will the happiness of others but not of oneself. We all already will our own happiness, Kant argues, and so it makes no sense to introduce an imperative for this. He also shows how Kantian ethics can accommodate our intuitions about supererogation—going beyond one's duty. Any act of beneficence indirectly fulfills our strict duty to make the happiness of others our end. There are many ways for an act of beneficence to have moral value under this duty, and some—the more demanding ones—belong to saints or heroes.

Hill concludes by addressing three difficulties. First, justice. In some cases the possession of wealth represents an injustice (Kant notes) that a government has failed to correct. Then the wealthy have a determinate duty of reparation. This is a matter of justice, not philanthropy. Second, priorities. Kantian morality, as Hill interprets it, requires that we give to worthy causes but gives no precise guidelines for what is worthy. Meeting the basic needs of others is worthy, but so is supporting education and the arts, which are important in Kant's larger conception of human dignity. Third is the problem of motive. Kant seems at times to argue that giving out of sympathy has no moral worth, but Hill shows why this is an oversimplification. Kant allows that sympathetic feelings have some value from a moral point of view.

2. Christine Swanton, "Virtue Ethics, Thick Concepts, and Paradoxes of Beneficence." Swanton introduces a theory that will be new to most readers of this volume: thick concept centralism (TCC), a species of virtue ethics. Thick concepts include loyalty, affability, love, and fairness. Thin concepts, such as right and wrong, are at best secondary to the thick concepts when they are exhibited virtuously. When is an act of loyalty virtuous? On Swanton's view

it is when the act hits the target of virtue—what Aristotle calls the mean. Swanton does not accept the agent-centered view that an act is virtuous when characteristic of a virtuous agent.

Her general thesis is that such a theory can resolve certain paradoxes of philanthropy. These paradoxes have arisen within what she calls the welfarist consequentialist tradition. This is the tradition which, setting virtues to one side, insists that morality consists in the promotion of the good, understood in terms of welfare. This tradition, which she opposes, depends on the use of thin moral concepts, such as right and wrong, and therefore stops at what she calls the simple thought that it's never right to prefer a worse state of affairs to a better.

Swanton's approach emphasizes the way in which we are situated with other people. We "have a need for bonding with others." We need to nurture the qualities on which communities depend, and these qualities include caring about individuals, groups, and projects that are special to us.

Using this theory Swanton shows how one can respond to a number of paradoxes: (1) Why does philanthropy seem overly demanding? Because people cling to the simple thought and do not temper it with respect for personal bonds. (2) Why does supererogation—going beyond one's duty—seem paradoxical? That is because we forget that a duty of virtue may be understood as "calibrated according to the nature and development of the agent." Saints and heroes go beyond duties calibrated in that way. (3) What are philanthropists to do when reason does not determine a course of action? Which charity to support? And by how much? Here she introduces the concept of narrative virtue: within a narrative context, one can be influenced virtuously by factors, such as bonds of love and loyalty, that are independent of optimizing welfare. (4) Why should I give if my gift literally makes no difference? In such a case it seems that I have no fair share to give, because even if I give, I have no share in the result. Swanton's answer is complex: failing to act in a "making no difference" case might be virtuous or vicious. To see the difference, we need to use thick concepts, and specifically to treat fairness as thick.

This is rich and productive theory. The layperson may find it harder than welfarism to understand but, at the same time, will recognize its results as more in line with everyday thinking about philanthropy.

3. Jeff McMahan, "Doing Good and Doing the Best." As a proponent of effective altruism, McMahan is disappointed with the result of his argument: when giving is supererogatory—that is, when it is not wrong not to give—he finds that it is not wrong to give ineffectively. So he challenges effective altruists to show "that much less of doing good is supererogatory than we have hitherto imagined." If Leona Helmsley would not do wrong in giving nothing for human welfare, then she does not do wrong in giving to the welfare of dogs in preference to human beings. McMahan looks closely at several proposed counterexamples to this result and draws a series of subtle but telling distinctions. We do find cases in which it appears wrong to do a lesser good, but those are cases in which one would incur no added cost in doing the greater good.

Leona Helmsley has an interest in the welfare of dogs that she would have to sacrifice if she diverted her legacy to human welfare. Sacrificing such an interest adds to the cost for her of doing something that (we have agreed at the outset) she is not obliged to do at all: philanthropy. The Helmsley case is extreme, but many of us have interests we support with charitable giving—such as in the arts or in education—knowing that we could do more measurable good if we gave more effectively. Are we doing wrong by giving to the arts?

McMahan's defense of Helmsley's choice hangs on his assumption, stated at the outset, that the funds in question are hers to give, both legally and morally. If they were hers legally but not morally, then she would have a moral obligation to give them where they morally belong; doing so is not supererogatory. Giving is supererogatory only with funds that are morally yours. McMahan brings us to the conclusion that we need to examine more closely the extent to which giving is supererogatory.

4. Elizabeth Ashford, "Severe Poverty as an Unjust Emergency." This essay is a major contribution to the debate over effective altruism—to the question whether it is better to correct structural injustice or to make up for its effects through individual donations. The effect of injustice between the first and third worlds has been severe poverty: the inability to afford a minimally nutritious diet along with other requirements for survival.

The issue is what are the duties of affluent agents—those who can afford to help those in severe poverty without jeopardizing their own or their dependents' interests. Effective altruists have been put on the defensive by advocates for correcting injustice. Ashford shows that the two sides should not be arguing as if there were competition between them. Effective altruism turns out to be an obligation of justice. Affluent agents have two kinds of duty arising from severe poverty: a duty to correct injustice and a backup duty to respond to severe poverty as an emergency. She uses Henry Shue's tripartite analysis of human rights to show that these duties are not only compatible but necessarily linked: "Affluent agents' duties to donate to NGOs should be understood as backup duties, which arise because the primary duties imposed by the human right to subsistence have been violated."

Ashford's chapter includes a thorough review of theoretical and practical objections to effective altruism, along with persuasive replies. Effective altruism as an emergency backup does not supplant or undermine other necessary interventions. The argument is too complex to summarize here; this is a major contribution to the subject and should be widely read.

5. Brandon Boesch, "Integrity, Identity, and Choosing a Charity." Boesch aims to show that there are good, nonarbitrary, nonutilitarian considerations that bear on selecting charities. He builds on a famous argument from Bernard Williams to the effect that personal integrity can count against utilitarian reasoning—as it does if I am called upon to prevent harm by violating a value to which I have committed my life. Boesch fleshes out the required notion of integrity through a theory of identity. On his view, an identity is something one chooses through action rather than a label one claims for oneself. To have an identity is to choose consistently to act on—or at least to take seriously—a certain set of reasons. Having an identity, he then suggests, is a way of instantiating a virtue.

On the theory he develops, you violate your identity only when you fail to take the relevant reasons into consideration. You might identify yourself with the cause of human rights but still give the lion's share of your donations to other causes, so long as you consider seriously the commitments that flow from your identification with rights. Charitable giving is especially important to questions of identity because often the only way busy people can express their ethical commitments is through giving. This factor has generally been overlooked in philosophical writing about philanthropy. It is not arbitrary for us to express ethical commitments or solidarity with minority causes by writing checks; there are sound ethical reasons for making gifts, whether or not they are effective. In the end, in an amusing but valuable coda, Boesch points out that certain strategies for fundraising (such as the famous ice bucket campaign) are challenges to integrity.

Boesch's chapter was presented to us through a nationwide contest for graduate students on the subject of philanthropy. We chose it because it was a well-argued and original essay on a topic in philanthropy that has otherwise been neglected.

6. William MacAskill, Andreas Mogensen, and Toby Ord, "Giving Isn't Demanding." You might have read to this point in the book and agreed that you have an obligation to give, so long as the obligation is not too demanding. But what is too demanding? Some readers have thought that Peter Singer's principles of sacrifice were two demanding. MacAskill and his colleagues introduce a very weak principle of sacrifice: 10 percent of income for most members of the rich world's middle class, to be given (in effect) as effective altruism. This principle, they argue, is not too demanding. They do not argue that this exhausts one's philanthropic duty.

Their argument is based on research on the effects of wealth on well-being. A small increase for the very poor can improve their well-being far more than a loss in the same amount would reduce the well-being of a donor from the rich world. In other words, the benefits that effective altruism brings are larger, and the costs smaller, than most people believe. This is eye-opening research, and its results need to be widely promulgated. Good-hearted readers, if they take this argument together with Ashford's, will surely resolve to increase their giving in coming years.

7. "Afterword: Justice and Charitable Giving." Not all that we count as charitable giving is philanthropic. Some of it is required by considerations of justice. Although some of these considerations point to effective altruism, as Ashford shows, some point in other directions. The wealth and happiness of many of us in the rich world are built on sacrifices that have been forced on others or that others have made. For such reasons we may have obligations of justice that compete with each other, as well as with philanthropic duties.

Philanthropic duties are wide and may be fulfilled in a number of ways. Duties of justice must be narrower; they must be fulfilled toward certain recipients and (in some cases) in certain amounts.

The afterword sketches the range of giving obligations we may have under justice, introduces fair share arguments, and discusses the problem of free-riders who may not wish to ride at all.

My part in this volume is dedicated to the memory of my father, Archibald M. Woodruff Jr. (1912–1984), who gave or left the bulk of his estate to charitable causes. Influenced by his example, and by arguments such as those found in these pages, I regularly give well over 10 percent of my income—although not entirely to the causes deemed most effective by effective altruists. The education that was given to me has made possible the life I have led and the money I have earned, so I have thought it right to give some money back to education—including to the study of philosophy at Oxford, where much of the best recent work on philanthropy has been done. I have also given selectively to the arts, for similar reasons. I find philanthropy a delicate topic, touching as it does on intimate issues of value and individual identity. As Boesch points out, donors' giving reflects their individual sense of who they are and where their obligations lie. Those who write about this topic should make their money follow their arguments. I have tried to do so.

FURTHER READING

The literature on the ethics of giving is growing rapidly. Here I list only the most important recent work.

Peter Singer started the current philosophical discussion of philanthropy with his 1972 article "Famine, Affluence, and Morality," which he followed with *The Life You Can Save* (2010). He made the case for effective altruism in *The Most Good You Can Do* (2015). In the same year William MacAskill published *Doing Good Better*, which carries the case for effective altruism further. A fine recent anthology of work by philosophers on this subject is *Giving Well: The Ethics of Philanthropy* (2011), edited by Patricia Illingworth, Thomas Pogge, and Leif Wenar. Judith Lichtenberg seeks a psychological motivation for philanthropy in *Distant Strangers: Ethics, Psychology, and Global Poverty* (2014). Julie Salamon's small book deserves a wide audience: *Rambam's Ladder: A Meditation on Generosity and Why It Is Necessary to Give* (2003). Karl Zinsmeister has written from a historical perspective about the value of philanthropy in *What Comes Next? How Private Givers Can Rescue America in an Era of Political Frustration* (2016). Full references to these works are appended to chapter 7 in this volume.

Chapter 1

Duties and Choices
in Philanthropic Giving

Kantian Perspectives

THOMAS E. HILL JR.

Why should the wealthy share their resources to improve the lives of others? Is philanthropy a duty, merely a morally optional personal choice, or something morally good to do but not a duty? If it is a duty, to what extent must one give? Does it matter what good cause a philanthropist contributes to? These are not easy questions in practice or in moral theory. Attempts to answer them lead us to more general questions. For example, why should anyone give their goods to others? How can we determine what, when, to whom, and how much we should give? Surely the context of the questioner matters, but which features of the context are relevant? Does it matter, for example, how relative wealth was acquired, whether the background institutions governing property are just, whether the gift will meet basic needs, whether the recipients are deserving, and whether the gift is well motivated? My aim here is to address some of these questions from a broadly Kantian point of view.

My plan is first to lay out what I take to be basic points in Kant's moral theory. This includes both his general principles regarding giving help to others and the abstract Kantian idea of the moral point of view from which we can critically assess more specific moral principles. Then I respond to several objections to the Kantian position as I understand it. These are (1) David Cummiskey's charge that on my interpretation Kant's duty to help others would be *anemic*, treating helping others as optional in cases where morality demands immediate action; (2) Michael Slote's complaint that the Kantian position *requires us to devalue our own happiness* relative to others and so to count ourselves as less important than others; and (3) J. O. Urmson's famous objection that Kantian ethics denies the reasonable commonsense idea that some saintly and heroic efforts to aid others are *supererogatory*—that is, good to do but *beyond duty*. Finally, I consider briefly how the Kantian perspective might apply to more specific questions about the nature and extent of the moral duty of the wealthy to support good causes. For example, in deciding how much we ought to give, does it matter *how wealth was acquired* and *whether those in need are deserving*? Is it more important to meet basic needs than merely to do favors? Why should we promote education and the arts rather than more frivolous pursuits? How, if at all, does it matter what our motives for giving are? Kant did not address all of these specific questions explicitly, but his moral theory has implications concerning them.

BACKGROUND AND THE SUPREME MORAL PRINCIPLE(S)

Kant's writings on ethics are many and spread over many years, and the commentaries on his work, sympathetic and critical, are vast and remarkably varied in their interpretations. For present purposes I cannot give due regard to all (or even the best) of these, but instead will just review some basic ideas, the structure of his moral theory, and his several formulations of the supreme moral principle. Then, in the next section, I will sketch my interpretation, or reconstruction, of the principle that I think combines the best of all of the formulations in a way that is relevant to more specific ethical questions, for example, our questions about philanthropic giving. My aim here is not to defend Kant but to lay out some main ideas and consider how a contemporary Kant*ian* theory might extend them.

We can distinguish two aspects of Kant's moral philosophy that correspond roughly to the familiar distinction between meta-ethics and normative ethics. Under the first heading (meta-ethics) we might classify Kant's *analysis* (or explanation) of common moral concepts (such as "ought" and "duty") and the special philosophical ideas that, in his view, they presuppose (for example, autonomy of the will). Kant's *arguments* to identify and "establish" the supreme moral principle may also be regarded as belonging to meta-ethics, and the same may be said of his heroic attempts to reconcile his ideas of a free and autonomous will with the presuppositions of empirical science. For our purposes, the most important points may be these:

1. Moral choices should be guided and constrained by respect for moral reasons, and these presuppose that reason-governed agents implicitly accept and, for the most part, follow some general principles of rational choice. Some of these, exemplified by (what I call) the Hypothetical Imperative, concern prudential and other instrumental choices. At least one other necessary rational principle, expressed in several

formulations of the Categorical Imperative, concerns morally required intentions and choices.

2. Moral principles are *imperative* for human beings and any others like us who are both capable of following rational principles and liable to violate them. Imperatives express the idea that one *ought* to act, even *must* act as rational principles prescribe.[1]

3. Moral imperatives, at least the most fundamental one(s), express the idea that one (rationally) must choose to act in certain ways and not because doing so promotes one's happiness or helps one to achieve one's personal ends. Being moral may promote one's own happiness, if one is lucky, but that is not why one should be moral.

4. The fundamental requirement of rationality expressed in the Categorical Imperative is supposed to be *a synthetic priori* principle (a "principle of *pure* practical reason"), but empirical facts are necessary and important in the specific application of moral principles to the human condition and to one's particular circumstances (*G* 220–221 [4: 419–420]).

5. Despite their emotional makeup and feelings on particular occasions of choice, any responsible moral agent must be presumed to have the capacity (or "freedom") to follow moral requirements when they recognize them, and they can see what is morally required at least regarding most important moral choices.

These *meta-ethical* aspects of Kant's moral philosophy are important, controversial, and challenging to scholars, but for present purposes it is best to concentrate on Kant's *normative* ethical theory. This includes both his well-known attempts to articulate the supreme moral principle in his *Groundwork for the Metaphysics of Morals* and his later efforts to draw out and illustrate the implications of the supreme moral principle for recurrent issues of justice and virtue in *The Metaphysics of Morals*. Kant argued that the supreme moral principle, which he expressed in his several formulations of the Categorical Imperative, is morally comprehensive, unconditionally rational, and presupposed in common moral understanding. When applied systematically to the human condition, taking into account our basic human needs, weaknesses, and vulnerabilities as well as our rational and moral capacities, the supreme moral principle prescribes certain more specific, but still quite abstract, principles of social justice and individual virtue for human beings. These principles express Kant's idea of the rational and reasonable standards for legal systems and international relations as well as for individual ethical decisions.

The fundamental requirements of morality are supposed to be summarized in three famous formulas (with some variations) (G 221–237 [4: 420–437]). Roughly the formula of universal law tells us to act only on maxims that we can will as universal laws. The humanity formula tells us to treat humanity, in each person, never simply as a means but always as an end in itself. The formula of the kingdom of ends says that we must act in accord with the laws of a possible kingdom of ends. Interpretations of the formulas and how they relate to one another have varied widely. Critics have pressed apparent objections, and Kantians have responded, often proposing helpful supplements and modifications.[2] Rather than trying to review this vast literature here, I will just summarize my reconstruction of Kant's basic framework for assessing more specific moral principles and their limits. This basic framework is supposed to guide and constrain our thinking about the purpose of charitable giving, the general obligation to promote the happiness of others, and the special duty to aid those in dire need.

A KANTIAN FRAMEWORK FOR THINKING ABOUT MORAL PRINCIPLES AND CHOICES

Arguably Kant's formulations of the Categorical Imperative are meant to express different aspects of a fundamental deliberative point of view. A formulation that combines ideas from the others is that *we should always conform to the laws of a possible kingdom of ends.* This ideal moral commonwealth is defined as a union of rational and autonomous persons under common moral laws of which they are both *authors* and *subjects.*[3] Members respect each other as "ends in themselves." Humanity in each person has dignity, an unconditional and incomparable worth. Humans have "autonomy of the will," and so as lawmakers they "abstract from personal differences" and legislate only laws that all can endorse. The most fundamental moral requirement is to conform to the more specific (or midlevel) principles that would be accepted by all the members of this ideal moral union. More generally the idea is that we should view such principles as authoritative insofar as they would be endorsed by and for all rational moral agents who, while setting aside their individual differences, aim to find principles that respect the *dignity* of humanity in each person. *Humanity* refers to a person's rational capacities—not simply to set oneself ends but also to think consistently, to understand facts, to coordinate one's ends and means, and to acknowledge, respect, and follow rational moral requirements whether or not they promote one's happiness or personal ends.[4] From these abstract ideas, I have often suggested, one can develop a Kant*ian* deliberative framework beyond Kant's texts, as a perspective for assessing specific moral principles, trying to reconcile potential conflicts, and deliberating about possible exceptions (Hill 2012, chapters 8, 10, 11, 14; Hill 2016).

The idea of moral legislation here has some apparent advantages over common interpretations of Kant's universal law and humanity formulations when these are taken by themselves.[5] For example, it encourages systematic thinking about how our moral norms work together. Without conflating law and ethics, we can see by analogy that we need to evaluate sets of rules and principles together. What might make sense as a "universal law" in the context of certain laws might be unacceptable in the context of other laws. For example, we may need more demanding requirements of personal aid to the needy if the laws of justice do not require governmental welfare. Thinking systematically also exposes potential conflicts among principles and invites wide-ranging critical reflection on how they should be managed. The analogy with law also suggests that legislators can continue to affirm the fundamental moral point of view as their constitution, as it were, while allowing reasonable limits and exceptions to specific rules. Besides that, in light of the many problems generated by attempts to test *maxims* by the formula of universal law, the legislative perspective is more promising too, because its application does not require us to pick out one most salient description of a person's acts and intentions to determine what is permissible. If, under any true description, the agent's intentional acts and policies are incompatible with the system of "legislated" moral principles, they would be forbidden, otherwise not. These principles are the moral "laws" or objective maxims that everyone ought to follow, and so it is wrong to act on any personal maxim that cannot be willed consistently with them.

To apply Kant's model charitably, we must not assume that the purpose is to find principles that are appropriate only for a utopian world wherein everyone always follows the principles. We are concerned with moral requirements for real people in the actual world, where many are weak and ignorant and some are corrupt and even evil. The model offers an *ideal* for how to articulate and assess midlevel moral principles for *imperfect* (nonideal) moral agents in an *actual* and dangerously imperfect world. In other words, we should think of the lawmakers when deliberating as wise, informed, consistent, and free from irrelevant biases, but they are reflecting on principles appropriate for themselves and others in actual human conditions where many are unwise, uninformed, inconsistent, and driven by personal biases. This does not mean that we should water down basic moral requirements to make them easy to follow without much thought or effort, but it must be possible for any competent adult to understand and follow them, and they should appropriately guide thoughtful and conscientious people as to how they should respond to the problems they face because others are too unthinking, lazy, weak, or corrupt to act rightly. To ignore the existence of these human limitations would be to construct an ethics for a world of enlightened angels. Our principles regarding how much we should give to charitable causes, for example, should not be framed in utter disregard of the probability that in fact not everyone will do "their fair share" to solve problems. This is not to excuse those who refuse to help but rather to acknowledge what should be obvious: that they contribute to the problems faced by those who want to do the right thing.

Another problem in trying to apply Kant's abstract model without adjustment is this: In Kant's ideal kingdom of ends all of the fully rational and autonomous moral lawmakers *agree* on the laws or principles that they legislate, but in the actual world, as we know, even the most conscientious deliberators often disagree. Kant's model of moral legislation, then, might be best construed as an ideal perspective for *conscientious* reflection on moral principles rather than as a procedure by which we can confidently determine an independent moral truth. If so, acknowledging that reasonable and well-meaning people often disagree, we would take it as *our standard for striving to do right* that we act consistently with principles that, *in our best judgment* after due consultation with others, we think that everyone who takes up the Kantian deliberative perspective should endorse and commend to others. In construing Kant*ian* theory in this modest way, we see it as *proposing* principles to guide and constrain moral decision-making and as *aspiring* to be worthy of the actual agreement of all reason-governed human beings, but not as insisting that actual agreement is necessary for the validity of its principles or as guides for conscientious decision-making.

KANT ON THE IMPERFECT DUTIES OF BENEFICENCE AND MUTUAL AID

In the Doctrine of Virtue (part II of *The Metaphysics of Morals*) Kant lays out his most comprehensive and systematic account of the more substantive moral principles that are supposed to apply to all (rationally competent) human beings.[6] These include principles of law and justice (*Recht*) concerning, for example, property, contracts, marriage, the provisions of a just constitution, the state's authority to coerce and punish, and international and cosmopolitan right. The substantive moral principles for all human beings include "duties to oneself" (regarding suicide, lying, servility, drunkenness, masturbation, and self-improvement) and "duties to others" (regarding respect, love, gratitude, friendship, etc.). Especially relevant to our topic are the duties of *practical love* for others, which include a general duty to promote others' happiness and (sometimes conflated) a more specific duty to aid those in distress (*MM* 198–208 [6: 448–461]). Because we cannot will to have affectionate love, our *duty* is only to have *practical love*, that is, to *act beneficently* toward others, no matter how we may happen to feel. The duty is to promote the *permissible* ends of others, and, assuming their ends are permissible, we are to contribute to their happiness as *they* conceive of it, not as we might define it. If we take the happiness of others seriously as an end, then we are not of course concerned simply to please them, do favors, and help them with their particular personal projects. More important is their having basic resources for survival and good health, opportunities for education and culture, and the security of a sustainable future for loved ones.

This general duty of beneficence is an *imperfect duty*, which means at least that it is not specific regarding how, when, and how much to help others.[7] Imperfect duties, in Kant's moral system, are constrained by stricter *perfect* duties of justice, self-respect, and respect for others. For example, often we may choose to give to this charity or that, to give money or time, and so on, but we must not try to get funds for charitable causes by stealing the justly acquired property of others or by deceiving, begging, or "sucking up" to potential donors in a degrading or servile way. And, importantly, we must not try to help others in ways that disrespect them or undermine their self-respect.

In Kant's moral system the wide imperfect duty *to act beneficently* stems from a strict duty of virtue (a categorical imperative) *to make the happiness of others an end* of one's own. In other words, although the general duty does not specify precisely how and to what extent we should help others, it is a *strict nonoptional duty* to include among one's personal ends a serious commitment to contribute to others' ability to achieve their own permissible ends. Being somewhat negligent about helping others does not make one a *vicious* person, but one would be vicious if one rejected the principle of beneficence, refusing to make it a serious end for oneself to promote the happiness of others (*MM* 153 [6: 390]).

A special case of beneficence is giving aid to those in distress, for example, those needing immediate help to meet basic needs for survival and tolerable existence. In this sort of context, presumably, one's duty to aid may become more determinate and strict than the general duty to promote others' happiness, in that refusal to give aid when one can easily (and when others cannot or will not) help must be judged wrong by direct appeal to the Categorical Imperative. The general imperfect duty to promote others' happiness by itself does not (and cannot) express all that Kantian ethics has to say about helping others. It states a minimum (though rock-bottom) requirement for everyone in all conditions: one must not be indifferent to others but treat their happiness as an end. But other considerations may be relevant. For example, in the immediately urgent emergency cases wherein I can easily help and no one else can or will, arguably my refusing aid would demonstrate insufficient regard for the humanity of those in need, even if I generally count the happiness of others as one of my ends. Kantian moral lawmakers are supposed to regard the humanity, or capacity for rational autonomous living, as an end in itself, something of unconditional and incomparable worth. Thus it seems presumptively wrong, contrary to the dignity of humanity, to let a person starve to death or live in mind-numbing squalor when one can easily prevent this by giving up relatively trivial things that have mere "price."

Apart from such emergency cases (local and global), are we at liberty (and not at fault) for showing partiality toward those we love when we choose *whose* happiness to promote? From a moral point of view no one's happiness is intrinsically more important than anyone else's, but this does not mean that each individual has an obligation to take up the point of view of an impartial even-handed god when helping others. After explaining that everyone should *wish* for the happiness of others ("taking delight in the well-being of every other"), Kant explains that the biblical command to love our neighbors as ourselves means *"practical* benevolence (beneficence), making the well-being and happiness of others my end" (my italics). He explains, "For in wishing I can be *equally* benevolent to everyone, whereas in acting I can, without violating the universality of the maxim, vary the degree greatly in accordance with the different objects of my love (one of whom concerns me more than another)" (*MM* 200–201 [6: 451–452]).

Thus partiality to family and friends is not objectionable, barring special circumstances, in fulfilling one's general duty of beneficence. And, contrary to some commentators, I think it is also clear that, barring emergencies, Kant thought that there is a wide area for permissible pursuit of one's own happiness and we need not always favor others when their permissible ends conflict with ours.

I turn next to several objections to Kant's position or to my understanding of it. David Cummiskey and Marcia Baron are sympathetic with Kant's position but partly disagree with my presentation of it, and Michael Slote and J. O. Urmson are critical of Kant as they understand him.

IS THE KANTIAN DUTY TO GIVE AID TOO ANEMIC?

In defending his "Kantian consequentialism," Cummiskey (1996, 219ff.) argues for what he calls a *robust* interpretation of Kant's principle of beneficence.[8] He acknowledges that the values associated with humanity (such as the ability to think, learn, reason, and set ends) should have priority over values that have mere "price" (such as material things and trivial pleasures). But, according to Cummiskey, the higher priority values are still commensurable with each other and should be promoted to the greatest extent possible.

Thus, not surprisingly, he regards the Kantian duty to give aid as very demanding, severely limiting the range of choices that are optional. By contrast, he argues, my reading of the duty is anemic, permitting far too many of our important choices to be optional.[9] A key example makes his point clearly. Suppose that while relaxing on the beach a strong swimmer sees a boat overturn and many people calling for help. He goes out with his small boat and rescues one person and then perhaps another, and after that, although he could easily rescue more, he stops and thinks, "I am required to help others to survive only sometimes and in some ways, and so I have done enough for today." The problem with my anemic interpretation, according to Cummiskey, is that it condones that sort of thinking.

I have disputed both Cummiskey's reading of Kant's texts and his understanding of the early (Hill 1971) article that he thought committed me to condoning the easygoing lazy rescuer. I will not repeat these textual points here, but simply explain our disagreement, as I see it. I agree that the rescuer in Cummiskey's story was wrong to rest content after a few rescues if he could easily have done more, and also I agree that we have reason to doubt any moral theory that condones his behavior and attitude. But my account of the Kantian duty to give aid does not have the objectionable implication. As I explained above and in "Meeting Needs and Doing Favors" (Hill 2002), Kant's *general* principle of beneficence, as presented most clearly in *The Metaphysics of Morals*, is a part of a system of moral principles meant to be applicable to all human beings in all circumstances. It cannot by itself determine in particular what is to be done in all cases of rescue, helping others, or giving to charity. Utilitarianism and other consequentialist theories often aspire to give what is at least in theory such a completely determinate guide, but Kant's general principle of beneficence is not supposed to be such a guide. It says that it is categorically imperative for everyone to adopt the happiness of others as an end but does not say specifically how and to what extent one must act to promote the happiness of others. It is not just that, as with all principles, *judgment* is required to apply it to particular circumstances, but more important, as a wide imperfect duty it leaves a certain "playroom" for free choice (*MM* 153 [6: 390]). We satisfy the general principle if we sincerely adopt the happiness of others as an end, incorporating it into plans and policies along with our other ends, moral and nonmoral. We must not be indifferent to the happiness of others, that is, to their achieving their own permissible personal ends, but the general principle does not by itself dictate specifically what we must do, when, or how much. Opportunities and resources to help others vary with circumstances, and other moral considerations may be relevant, such as justice, obligations of family and friendship, respect for human dignity, gratitude, and one's own welfare and legitimate aspirations.

The general principle of beneficence, then, may not *by itself* strictly determine either that the lazy rescuer had a duty to save more people or that he was permitted to quit after rescuing only a few. His quitting, however, suggests that he may have failed even to adopt the happiness of others as an end, and if so, he rejected the principle of beneficence and so was wrong (even vicious). But there is more to consider: Why did he quit? Was he in a hurry to go to a party, or just to rest comfortably and watch TV? If so, he has the wrong priorities. The Categorical Imperative implies that humanity in persons has dignity, a value that is above all price. For the lazy rescuer to let the drowning people die just for the sake of fun or comfort seems clearly to violate the Kantian priorities. Other factors too may be relevant, but the general point is that the principle of beneficence expresses just one important but indeterminate moral requirement for everyone, not a decision procedure for all cases where there is an opportunity to help others.

At times in *The Metaphysics of Morals* Kant seems to invoke a more specific principle regarding helping others, namely, that when we find another in dire distress and we can help at little cost to ourselves, then we ought to help, assuming there are no special overriding or excusing conditions (*G* 224 [4: 423]; *MM* 202 [6: 453]). This is a principle of ordinary morality, I think, and is roughly what Rawls (1999, 297–298) called the *principle of mutual aid*. This principle of mutual aid is more determinate than the general principle of beneficence and seems sufficient to condemn the lazy rescuer, but of course even this cannot by itself settle all cases.[10] As Jonathan Dancy (2004) often reminds us, particular circumstances may strengthen or "defeat" the judgments that our principles initially seem to recommend. Dancy doubts that we can always identify these "defeaters" and simply add them to our general principles as built-in exceptions. I will not try to do that, but later I will mention some factors in Kant's ethics that could justify variations in how his principles of beneficence and mutual aid apply to particular circumstances. This is not to say that all variations can be codified precisely but only that Kantian ethics can acknowledge significant complications when we try to judge what, how much, and to whom we ought to give aid.

MUST WE REGARD OTHERS' HAPPINESS AS MORE IMPORTANT THAN OUR OWN?

Slote (1992, 4–57, 98) raises an objection to Kant's position that may have troubled others as well.[11] He notes that Kant says we have a *direct* duty to promote others' happiness but only a quite limited and *indirect* duty to promote our own happiness. Slote infers that Kant requires us to devalue our own happiness relative to others, treating ourselves as if we are less important than others, and we can agree that this would be objectionable. Slote realizes, of course, that Kant's principles impose a *direct* duty on *other people* to promote *our* happiness but only an *indirect* duty to promote their own, but even this (he argues) is objectionable because it asks *everyone* to subordinate themselves to others in their efforts to promote happiness.

This subordination would be objectionable, I think, but it does not square with Kant's repeated insistence on moral equality of all persons and the duty to avoid servility. Slote's objection, I think, rests on several misunderstandings. One's limited duty to promote one's *own* happiness is *indirect* because being miserable undermines one's ability and will to fulfill *one's other duties*—to oneself and to others. In effect, the argument that we morally ought to attend to our own happiness treats this not as *in itself* a moral end but rather simply as a means or enabling condition for us to fulfill our *other* duties. One must not let oneself fall into a miserable condition that makes it difficult, if not impossible, to meet one's obligations or to avoid various vices. An indirect duty, in Kant's view, is not necessarily less stringent or important than a direct duty because Kant says that it is an *indirect* (ethical) duty to conform to the perfect (juridical) duties of justice, whereas the less strict and determinate (imperfect) requirements to improve one's mind and to be grateful to others are *direct* duties (*MM* 20–22 [6: 218–221]).

Also Kant's reason for saying that we do not have a direct duty to promote our own happiness is not that we should regard our own happiness as less important than others' but rather that *by natural necessity* we already care about our own happiness. In particular cases, of course, concern for one's own happiness may be outweighed, overshadowed, suspended, or temporarily lost in depression, but insofar as one's own happiness (as an end) is just the *general* end to realize all one's *particular* nonmoral personal ends, only those so deeply depressed that they care about nothing could lack happiness as an end altogether.[12]

In addition a supposed duty to promote one's own happiness that is parallel to the duty to promote others' happiness would be incoherent. If we spelled out such a *supposed* direct duty to promote one's *own* happiness it would be roughly this: "It is a moral imperative for everyone to adopt their own happiness as an end, and so they must will to promote their own (permissible) ends sometimes, somehow, and to some extent, and *at least if they so choose.*" According to Kant, everyone *inevitably* wills their own happiness as an end, but it cannot be a duty to do what one will inevitably do anyway. All the more because we should not try to help others with their personal projects if they are unwilling, the supposed parallel duty of beneficence to oneself would have to allow that the potential benefactor (oneself) should not help the potential beneficiary (oneself) if the beneficiary (again oneself) chooses to decline the aid. In effect, the supposed but incoherent direct duty to promote one's own happiness would tell me, "It is my duty, but I don't have to do it if I choose not to." Kant may not explicitly say that, barring special circumstances, we should not help others against their will, but it is likely that he took it for granted. I mention the point because it helps to explain why Slote's objection is mistaken, but it is also important for our broader discussion because too often well-meaning philanthropists try to make people in other cultures happy in ways they would refuse if they were given a choice.

CAN PROMOTING OTHERS' HAPPINESS BE GOOD TO DO BUT BEYOND DUTY?

In his classic essay "Saints and Heroes," J. O. Urmson (1958) raised the objection that Kant's ethics cannot accommodate the commonsense thought that some saintly and heroic acts are good and morally commendable even though the agent was not morally required to do them. Urmson acknowledges that some deeds are regarded as saintly and heroic because they are instances of *doing one's duty* in extraordinarily trying circumstances or with exceptional grace, but he calls our attention to other cases where the admirable acts are clearly beyond what anyone could demand or blame a person for not doing. Some philosophers classify such acts in the wider category of the *supererogatory*, which can include doing minor favors, such as giving an especially pleasing gift to a friend. The apparent problem is that Kant *seems* to deny that acts could be *morally good* to do if they are *not duties* that we *must* fulfill. He insists that moral education should not appeal to examples of superheroic acts, and famously he denies that any act can have *moral worth* if it is not done *from duty* (1997b, 127–128 [5: 155]; G 199–201 [4: 397–399]). What is "good" to do is what reason prescribes, and what is unconditionally good to do is *categorically* imperative for us as imperfectly rational beings. And Kantian ethics does not propose, prior to the standards of rational willing, any independent substantive goal (such as the greatest happiness or most intrinsically valuable universe) that could determine what is duty or "good to do beyond duty."

The issues here, however, are more complex than they first appear. In a very early essay (Hill 1971) I attempted to find the place in Kant's ethics that most closely approximates the common thought that some acts are good to do but not strictly required by duty. The kinds of acts that best fit this description, I suggested, are the acts of someone (i) who has sincerely and conscientiously (i.e., "from duty") adopted the happiness of others as an end, (ii) who for this reason has regularly and vigorously worked to improve the lives of others, (iii) who then does a favor to someone who is not in special need because he has conscientiously adopted the happiness of others as an end, (iv) in a context where strict duties of justice, respect, and so on neither require nor forbid the act, and (v) his contribution was beyond what most people would expect or would do. Such acts seem morally "good to do" in two ways. First, they intentionally promote a morally prescribed (though somewhat indeterminate) end, using morally permissible ends, doing what the recipient had no antecedent *right* to demand or expect. Second, by hypothesis, the ultimate motive is duty, and so, it seems, the acts are *morally worthy*. Because the general duty of beneficence does not specify when, how, or to what extent one is to promote the happiness of others, the *particular acts* in the specified contexts were *not required*—the agents had already sincerely adopted the end and could have promoted others' happiness in many different ways. Thus there is a sense in which the agents went "beyond duty" in doing the favors. A similar case, with some qualifications, might be made for saying that some (more serious) heroic or saintly acts are "beyond duty."

But, as I noted in the early essay, the problem is that if the beneficent agents are aware that their *particular* acts are not strictly required, then it *seems* that they cannot be acting *from duty*, and so their acts cannot have *moral worth*. So it seems that, after all, the special acts cannot be "morally *good* to do" in that sense, and therefore they cannot be "morally good to do but not required."

Marcia Baron welcomed this inference and argued that Kant has no place in his ethics for the idea of supererogation—and rightly so.[13] She proposes that the phenomena that prompt us to speak *as if* acts can be *good but beyond duty* can usually be expressed better by describing the virtues displayed in the especially commendable acts, for example, using such terms as "*remarkable* generosity, *uncommonly* thoughtful, and *unbelievably* courageous." The problem remains, however, that acts display *virtues* in Kant's sense because they manifest *strength of will in fulfilling duties*. So "remarkable generosity" would manifest one's *unwavering will to overcome any obstacle to fulfill one's duty* to share one's resources; "unbelievable courage" would be an incredible *fortitude of will to resist fear in order to do one's duty*; and so on. Display of extraordinary virtue in this sense is not what we ordinarily have in mind when we speak of acts that are *good to do but beyond duty*. For this reason I am not convinced by Baron's suggestion that Kantian ethics can simply use virtue terms to express (or replace) the idea that acts can be morally good but not required, commendable but not done from a (perhaps misplaced) sense of duty.

In "Meeting Needs and Doing Favors" (215–218) my alternative to Baron's proposal, perhaps stretching Kant's texts, was to say that Kantian theory can allow that acts can count as morally worthy if they are done *indirectly* from duty, that is, for the sake of an indeterminate end that one adopted and continues to affirm because it is a morally necessary end. If so, a beneficent act could be morally worthy (or good) even though there were many other ways to satisfy the end and so the particular act was not strictly required. A reasonably modified Kantian ethics, I suggested, should include in its system not only principles that say what is strictly required but also principles that say what kinds of acts are to be encouraged and commended (as "good to do") even though they are not strictly necessary.

COMPLICATING FACTORS

Much more needs to be said on these issues, but for now I turn briefly to consider factors that may affect how Kant's general ideas about beneficence apply to particular cases. These factors are, first, the considerations of justice, second, the importance of the benefits provided, and third, the benefactor's motives.

The Relevance of Justice in Particular Contexts

It is obvious that considerations of justice constrain the way we should give help to others, but how? Some points seem clear enough. Most obviously, Kant held that we should not use unjust means in our efforts to promote happiness. Legitimate states, even if imperfectly just, impose enforceable perfect juridical duties that define particular rights that individuals have a (presumably) perfect (but indirect) ethical duty to respect. General beneficence is only a wide imperfect duty, and one must not violate a perfect duty simply to further the happiness of others. There are exceptions to the duty to obey the law, but only when the authorities command us to do something in violation of strict duties, such as bearing false witness. This, I take it, is an example of what he calls "intrinsically immoral" or "contrary to inner morality" (*MM* 98 [6: 321–322], 136–137 [6: 371]). The general point that we should avoid using unjust means to promote happiness is relatively uncontroversial, though in hard cases one may hesitate to accept the absolute priority of justice over beneficence that seems to be a structural feature of Kant's system.

More controversial is whether the rich whose wealth was acquired by unjust means are required by justice to give substantially *as reparations* to those disadvantaged by their own unjust acts or by the past injustices from which they profited, in order to acknowledge the injustice, express remorse, and try to repair the damage. Most of us would probably agree that Andrew Carnegie, J. D. Rockefeller, and J. P. Morgan were *morally* obliged to share the wealth they acquired with callous disregard for the harm they caused, and many would add that they should have been legally obliged to do so. Kant's system can perhaps account for duties of reparation if they are strictly defined within a given system of legal rights, but I suspect that our intuitions here depend on a more expansive account of justice than we can find in Kant. Regarding the *ethical* duties that come with great wealth, Kant says that when people are very rich, having far more than they need, they should not see their giving aid to others as *meritorious* but as something they owe (*MM* 202–203 [6: 453–454]). Moreover Kant adds that since great wealth is often the result of injustices of government, it is questionable whether a rich person's aid to the needy is really philanthropy, that is, a gift rather than an obligation.

Priorities in Philanthropic Giving: Basic Needs versus Education, the Arts, and Entertainment

It should be clear from the summaries above, especially from Kant's ideas about the moral imperative to value humanity as an end in itself, that basic needs for a rational autonomous person among others should generally take priority over more insignificant concerns when one is deciding how to fulfill one's general duty of beneficence, other things being equal, but we have no precise guidelines here. For Kant there are no values, not even the value of humanity in persons, that individuals must (or even can) aggregate and try to maximize (even with "side constraints"). The second-order principles that distribute responsibility for promoting and preventing outcomes, a Kantian might say, are those that the Kantian legislators would prescribe for everyone, taking into account many factors, normative and empirical, relevant from that general perspective. One best respects humanity in each person by adhering to the principles that each would endorse when taking up that viewpoint. One's duties to oneself, Kant says, are the foundation of all duties, and so one must not degrade oneself and must be ready to reciprocate with others, accepting the principles that everyone with such priorities ideally would endorse. This is all very abstract, of course, and what responsibilities the system of Kantian principles would assign to each person remains open to argument. Kant thought that no one should commit murder but not that we are just as responsible to prevent loss of life. We should help police to prevent murders when we can and contribute to life-saving famine relief when needed, surely, but this does not mean we must devote all of our philanthropic efforts to these causes rather than, for example, education and the arts. These too are worthy causes. Appreciation of art and natural beauty are valuable expressions of human spirit and imagination that involve a detachment from mundane concerns that can prepare the way for moral attitudes. Education promotes knowledge useful for many purposes, and it can help people to escape superstition and conformity, drudgery and stagnant minds (Kant 1997a).

How Do Motives Affect the Worth of the Giver and the Gift?

In *The Metaphysics of Morals* Kant says that we should strive to fulfill all of our duties *from duty*. This is what a perfectly virtuous person would do, but because of human frailty, we human beings can only strive to do so (*MM* 196–197 [6: 446–447]). In the *Groundwork*, Kant argues for the seemingly more radical thesis that only acts done from duty have *moral worth* (*G* 199–201 [4: 397–399]). Acts done from sympathetic feelings, or even mixed motives, are said to have no moral worth. Does this mean that we should expunge our sympathetic feelings for the less fortunate and never praise and encourage those who help others from pity and kindness? Does it mean that unless we experience our giving as a strict demand, contrary to what we want to do, we may as well give up philanthropy or treat it as a morally optional hobby? No, to draw these messages from Kant's (admittedly controversial) claims would be a serious mistake.

First, in the *Groundwork* Kant focuses on acts done from duty, in contrast to acts merely in accord with duty, because they exemplify a *good* will, which is fully committed to duty, and his aim is to find the basic principle of such a will (*G* 193 [4: 392], 202–203 [4: 401–402]). Acts done from sympathy and mixed motives do not manifest a pure good will, as Kant understands this, and so they are not worthy of praise *as acts based on respect for moral law*. Such acts do not represent Kant's ideal of morally worthy motivation. Nevertheless, whether or not we have sympathy, it is still our duty to make the happiness of others an end and to aid the less fortunate. If we do not do this, we are not even acting "in accord with duty." Second, in *The Metaphysics of Morals* Kant acknowledges that sympathetic feelings can be helpful in combating our selfish tendencies (*MM* 204–206 [6: 456–458]). As we strive to improve in virtue, we must try to cultivate sympathetic regard for the less fortunate because this helps to clear away the selfish feelings that are obstacles to fulfilling our responsibilities, as we should, from respect for moral principle. Sympathetic feelings, then, are not without value from a moral point of view. We should try to cultivate them, and we can admire those who successfully cultivate them *for having personal traits that we should all wish and aim to have*. Third, the morally important motive of duty is a wholehearted commitment to acting rightly, and this need not be at work only in teeth-gritting efforts to do what we dislike doing. Good people will stand ready to resist temptations as necessary, but there is no reason to suppose that they can act from respect for moral principles only when they feel disinclined to do what they should. All the more, it is not necessary, possible, or desirable to keep a philosopher's abstract formula of the moral law before our minds as we avoid injustice and help the unfortunate. The basic moral standards, in Kant's view, are evident enough to all moral agents, whether good or bad. Also, arguably our commitment to morality can and should serve to shape our lives in a comprehensive and often indirect way, not necessarily as a motivating thought immediately accompanying every good act (Herman 2007).

NOTES

1. Kant (2003), *Groundwork for the Metaphysics of Morals* (hereafter abbreviated *G*), 214–218 [4: 413–417]. Bracketed numbers refer to the volume and page numbers in the standard Prussian Academy edition of Kant's works.
2. Some different interpretations of Kant's formulas, especially as they bear on beneficence, are described in Hill 2012, 35–70.
3. An exception is that the "head" of the kingdom of ends, lacking human needs and imperfections, is not *subject* to the laws but necessarily conforms. This is a reference to God, or a "holy will," who formally shares a traditional characteristic of sovereignty (author, not subject to the laws) but necessarily wills the same laws as the other rational autonomous legislating members and so is not said to be *bound* or under *obligation* because of them (*G* 234 [4: 433–434]).
4. One's reasonable interest in personal ends is subject to the qualification *insofar as these are compatible with the fundamental principles that all can endorse*. The moral perspective derived from Kant's kingdom of ends formula, as described in my summary expression, is meant to use an analogy, as Kant says, to bring the moral law "nearer to feeling" and "closer to intuition" (*G* 237 [4: 436]).
5. These putative advantages are noted in my old essay "The Kingdom of Ends" (Hill 1972).
6. Kant (1996), *The Metaphysics of Morals*, hereafter abbreviated *MM*.
7. As Marcia Baron emphasizes, the latitude allowed by different imperfect duties may vary significantly. The imperfect duties to promote the happiness of others and to develop one's mind and body are different in this respect from the imperfect duty to improve in moral virtue.

8. My discussions of Cummiskey and Baron are in Hill 2002.

9. To be fair, I should note that Cummiskey was responding to my earlier paper (Hill 1971), which did not fill out the explanation of Kant's position as I have above. I do not think that my earlier essay was subject to Cummiskey's objection, but it is understandable that it may have seemed that it did.

10. The principle of mutual aid may be too weak to explain why sometimes one must make serious sacrifices in order to help others in distress. In particular emergencies where no one else is in a position to rescue someone in distress, as in the lazy swimmer example, the values encapsulated in the Kantian idea of human dignity may demand that we give aid even at substantial cost to ourselves.

11. I discuss Slote's objection in Hill 1999.

12. The idea of happiness here is roughly what Kant describes at G 216–220 [4: 415–419], but in other passages it is treated as durable contentment. See, for example, G 195 [4: 393].

13. Marcia Baron's position on these matters is presented in several works: Baron 1995, 2015; Baron and Seymour Fahmy 2009.

REFERENCES

Baron, Marcia (1995). *Kantian Ethics (Almost) without Apology*. Ithaca, NY: Cornell University Press.

Baron, Marcia (2015). "The Supererogatory and Kant's Imperfect Duties." In Mark Timmons and Robert Johnson (eds.), *Reason, Value, and Respect: Themes from the Philosophy of Thomas E. Hill, Jr*. Oxford: Oxford University Press, 215–231.

Baron, Marcia and Melissa Seymour Fahmy (2009) "Beneficence and Other Duties of Love in *The Metaphysics of Morals*." In Thomas E. Hill Jr. (ed.), *The Blackwell Guide to Kant's Ethics*. Oxford: Wiley-Blackwell, 211–228.

Cummiskey, David (1996). *Kantian Consequentialism*. New York: Oxford University Press.

Dancy, Jonathan (2004). *Ethics without Principles*. Oxford: Oxford University Press.

Herman, Barbara (2007). "Making Room for Character." In Barbara Herman (ed.), *Moral Literacy*. Cambridge, UK: Cambridge University Press, 1–28.

Hill, Thomas E., Jr. (1971). "Kant on Imperfect Duty and Supererogation." *Kant-Studien* 62 (1–4): 55–76. Reprinted in Thomas E. Hill Jr. (1992), *Dignity and Practical Reason in Kant's Moral Theory*. Ithaca, NY: Cornell University Press, 157–177.

Hill, Thomas E., Jr. (1972). "The Kingdom of Ends." In Lewis White Beck (ed.), *Proceedings of the Third International Kant Congress*. Dordrecht: Reidel.

Reprinted in Thomas E. Hill Jr. (1992), *Dignity and Practical Reason in Kant's Moral Theory*. Ithaca, NY: Cornell University Press, 58–66.

Hill, Thomas E., Jr. (1999). "Happiness and Human Flourishing in Kant's Ethics." *Social Philosophy and Policy* 16 (1): 143–175. Reprinted in Thomas E. Hill Jr. (2002), *Human Welfare and Moral Worth*. New York: Oxford University Press, 182–191.

Hill, Thomas E., Jr. (2002). "Meeting Needs and Doing Favors." In Thomas E. Hill, Jr. (ed.), *Human Welfare and Moral Worth*. Oxford: Oxford University Press, 201–243.

Hill, Thomas E., Jr. (2012). *Virtues, Rules, and Justice: Kantian Aspirations*. Oxford: Oxford University Press.

Hill, Thomas E., Jr. (2016). "Human Dignity and Hard Choices." *Proceedings and Addresses of the American Philosophical Association* 89, 74–94.

Kant, Immanuel (1996). *The Metaphysics of Morals*. Edited by Mary Gregor. Cambridge, UK: Cambridge University Press.

Kant, Immanuel (1997a) An Answer to the Question: What Is Enlightenment? In *Practical Philosophy*. Translated and edited by Mary Gregor. Cambridge, UK: Cambridge University Press, 11–22.

Kant, Immanuel (1997b). *Critique of Practical Reason*. Edited by Mary Gregor. Cambridge, UK: Cambridge University Press.

Kant, Immanuel (2003). *Groundwork for the Metaphysics of Morals*. Translated and edited by Thomas E. Hill Jr. and Arnulf Zweig. Oxford: Oxford University Press.

Rawls, John (1999). *A Theory of Justice*. Cambridge, MA: Harvard University Press.

Slote, Michael (1992). *From Morality to Virtue*. New York: Oxford University Press.

Urmson, J. O. (1958). "Saints and Heroes." In A. I. Melden (ed.), *Essays in Moral Philosophy*. Seattle: University of Washington Press, 198–216.

Chapter 2

Virtue Ethics, Thick Concepts, and Paradoxes of Beneficence

CHRISTINE SWANTON

Reasons of beneficence are at the core of ethics, and also alas, many of its most intractable theoretical problems, indeed paradoxes. We have paradoxes of supererogation, problems of extreme demandingness, underdetermination of choice of, for instance, charitable endeavor by reasons, the "It makes no difference whether or not I do it" paradox of "pooled beneficence" (Cullity 2000). All of these paradoxes are discussed below. What is needed for the resolution of these problems, I argue, is an appreciation of the distinctive nature of what McDowell has called the ethical mode of access to the real, what he calls the *logos* of ethics. In brief, that mode is seen as openness to an ethical reality of notably (but among other things) reasons, reasons identified in a rich and situated way through what has been called the thick concepts, such as kind, generous, caring, nonmanipulative, humiliating, callous, and so forth. That openness constitutes the mode of being of that reality and thereby its ontology. The second half of this chapter applies this idea to reasons of beneficence in the context of paradoxes of practical rationality.

To date, what might be called the ethics of beneficence has been largely dominated by the relatively thin and nonevaluative concepts that pervade the welfarist consequentialist tradition. Three core ideas animate this tradition.

1. Morality essentially concerns welfare (Welfarist Morality).
2. Welfare is understood in a way that is not essentially aretaic (Aretaic Independence of Welfare).
3. The moral agent is bound to maximize the good (understood in welfarist terms). This thesis is itself underpinned by three theses:

   3a. The only right-making relation is that of promotion (the Hegemony of Promotion).
   3b. It can never be right to prefer a worse state of affairs to a better (the Simple Thought).[1]
   3c. We regard as better a state of affairs in which there is more value rather than less value (the More Is Better thesis).

The modern virtue ethical tradition since Anscombe's famous 1958 paper has had a hand in questioning all these theses. Philippa Foot (1985) has attacked the Simple Thought and the More Is Better thesis. Virtue ethical theory is a thoroughgoing critique of the Aretaic Independence of Welfare. My book *Virtue Ethics: A Pluralistic View* (Swanton 2003) includes a sustained attack on the hegemony of promotion thesis. Bernard Williams (1985) questions the narrow conceptions of the moral, which have so blighted the analytic tradition, with his notion of the ethical, understood through the thick evaluative concepts.

THICK CONCEPT CENTRALISM

Virtue ethics shares Williams's view about the centrality of the thick concepts in ethics. The aim of this chapter is to outline and defend a virtue ethical version of that view, what I shall call thick concept centralism (TCC), applying it to reasons of beneficence. For the purposes of this chapter, the defense is not thoroughgoing, but the next section provides some needed background to the metaphysical basis of and nature of TCC. Defense of TCC is more of the "proof of the pudding is in the eating" kind: I deploy TCC to show that reducing ethical thought to nonevaluative or normatively thin concepts causes paradoxes that are resolvable through TCC.

What, then, is TCC? TCC is defined by two theses.

Centrality of Thick Concepts:

The thick evaluative notions are central to ethics in this sense. Within the network of concepts denoting features that are reasons, relatively nonevaluative features such as helping, giving pleasure, satisfying preferences, and benefiting (broadly reasons of beneficence) need to be further conceptualized by a large range of thick evaluative concepts such as kind, callous, generous, humiliating, and manipulative for their reason-giving status to be properly assessed.

Here is just one example from the ethics of beneficence. What leads to extreme demandingness is "the simple impartialist thought that each person is equally real and that each successive person who generates demands on the benevolent agent does so iteratively" (Thomas 2006, 133.) This impersonal conception is devoid of the human-specific meaning provided by the reason-supplying status of thick concepts, with their emotional conditions of intelligibility, in particular those relating to domains of human concern such as bonds with near and dear, one's own projects, and so on. If reasons of beneficence and their demands are understood through a large range of irreducibly normative virtue and vice concepts dealing with those concerns, we can see how extreme demandingness may be undercut. In a virtue ethical form of the Centrality of Thick Concepts thesis, the evaluative shape provided by our grasp of thick concepts is a precondition of further assessment of, for instance, benefiting or helping by the complex standards determining the virtuousness of the benefiting or helping.[2]

The second thesis (somewhat confusingly for our purposes) is what Susan Hurley has called noncentralism. This thesis makes a connection between reasons for action specified through thick concepts and right action. This next thesis I call noncentralism:

Noncentralism:

"Non-centralism about reasons for action rejects the view that the general concepts of *right* and *ought* are logically prior to and independent of specific reason giving concepts such as *just* and *unkind*." (Hurley 1985, 56)[3] Assuming that not all kind, patient, loyal, honest, courageous, and so forth acts are virtuous or right, we need to assess such reasons in terms of standards that allow the predication of "virtuous" or "right" to actions so described.

The next section elucidates TCC further by locating it within an objectivist realist metaphysical conception that has its roots in the work of Heidegger but is essentially McDowellian. According to this conception, there are ethical facts but not facts existing wholly independent of the sensibilities, constructive imagination, and interpretation of agents. John McDowell has done ethics a huge service by arguing that ethics is both irreducibly normative and naturalistic within a realist conception. A major thrust of his work is to argue against restrictive conceptions of naturalism that tie the concept to the understandings of the natural sciences. In his "Two Sorts of Naturalism" (1995, 164) he claims the following:

> It is one thing to recognize that the impersonal stance of scientific investigation is a methodological necessity for the achievement of a valuable mode of understanding reality; it is quite another thing to take the dawning grasp of this, in the modern era, for a metaphysical insight into the notion of objectivity as such, so that objective correctness in any mode of thought must be anchored in this kind of access to the real.

In particular, he argues, ethics is a *distinctive* mode of access to the real that is irreducibly normative and that can provide "objective correctness," secured on his view through the distinctive orientation of virtue. What is the nature of the distinctively ethical mode of access to the real? This question is really two:

1. What is a "mode of access to the real"?
2. What is the nature of the distinctively *ethical* mode of access to the real?

THE METAPHYSICS OF THICK CONCEPT CENTRALISM

An answer to the first question takes us into the metaphysics of the ethical. McDowell's views are not well understood, largely because he is often misinterpreted as speaking of concepts or epistemology rather than ontology. In particular, to understand what is going on in the quoted passage we need to know what McDowell means by "access" in its ontological as opposed to an epistemological sense. We need to understand how and why the more basic notion of access—openness to the world—yields an ontology. Ontology, then, is not simply the entities that exist, but entities that exist *as* meaningfully engaged with by human beings. Properties are attributed to entities within a framework of significance relations, whether of ethics, art, productions, equipment. In this way openness through the framework of significance relations constitutes the "being" or ontology of an entity, and as McDowell suggests, there may be more than one mode of openness and thereby more than one mode of being, modes such as the mathematical, the ethical, and so on.

Two notions of access must thus be distinguished: the epistemic and something more basic. The more basic notion is "openness to the world" such that it is made intelligible through conceptualization, as opposed to "merely inhabiting an environment," a distinction McDowell (2007, 343) attributes to Heidegger. Indeed, we need to disambiguate not only the notion of access but also that of understanding. "Understanding," like "access," is ambiguous between intelligibility and justified belief; between our intentional access to properties of a certain broad type such as the ethical, which is needed for the ethical to exist, and an epistemic notion whereby our openness to, for instance, virtue or virtuous action has to be justified as accurate. As McDowell (1994, 82) puts it, once our eyes are opened to the practical ethical world (constituting the intelligibility of ethics as something that is open to us) epistemology takes over: "Thereafter our appreciation of its detailed layout is indefinitely subject to refinement, in reflective scrutiny of our ethical thinking."

In line with both Heidegger's and McDowell's terminology, the regulating structure or significance relations constituting the distinctively ethical mode of access to the real will, for simplicity of reference, be called the *logos* of ethics: "The original meaning of *logos* is . . . the connecting, the relationship . . . what holds together that which stands within it. . . . *Logos* is the regulating structure."[4] Things are accessed (in the sense of intentionally accessed) through what Heidegger calls the "a as b" structure (see Heidegger 1995, 436): "the 'as' is the basic structure whereby we understand and have access to anything."[5] "That which stands within it" (the *logos*) are the things, a, "which are held together" through b. A *particular logos* renders things significant *as* b.

According to this picture, there is a two-way ontological dependence between modes of intentional access and entities. In the case of ethics it admits ethical facts but not facts existing wholly independently of the sensibilities of agents. But not just sensibilities as if we were simply passive observers of ethical facts, like the brownness and hardness of tables. Iris Murdoch, also a realist in this vein, emphasized the correct emotional orientation, constructive imagination, and interpretative effort needed as part of our openness to entities. Furthermore in this two-way ontological dependence there is no ontological primacy. Heidegger (1994, 18–19) puts the point by claiming that openness is "fourfold," including the "thing [being] open to us" and "we [being] open to the thing,"[6] which is a "unity" that nonetheless permits of analytical separation. That is, although aspects of "the four-fold unitary openness" are separately describable for the purposes of understanding them, they are not separate *in re*.

To understand two-way ontological dependence, consider an approach to the ethics of responsiveness to the other, whether in philanthropy or refraining from killing. Levinas emphasizes the other being open to us: the face of the other is the origin of a command to us, but "the call of the other is not heard through any prior phenomenological, hermeneutical or even theological lens, but is the very origin and ground of being, language, and action as such" (Wall 2005, 122). Levinas has been criticized for not appreciating the nature of the responsiveness of she to whom the command is addressed, but if the addressee is not herself open to the other because of unspeakable cruelty and callousness or even complete indifference, the "call" of the other will not be intelligible as an ethical command. Ricoeur, by contrast, has been criticized for not appreciating adequately the other's being open to us as origin of the command, thinking too strongly of the nature of the addressee's giving the other the "gift" of love (Wall 2005, 124).

VIRTUE ETHICS AND THE THICK CONCEPTS

We turn now to our answer to the second question: What is the nature of the distinctively *ethical* mode of access to the real? Here is the brief answer: The regulating structure or significance relations constituting the distinctively ethical mode of access to the real—the *logos* of ethics—is described at the most fundamental level by TCC. The thick concepts are central to ethics in a metaphysical sense; that is, they are central to the *logos* of ethics.

How in particular do the thick concepts "anchor ethical thought to the real," as McDowell puts it (in the above quote, 1995, 164), within the *logos* of ethics?

There are several issues that need to be addressed in order for us to have an adequate conception of this anchoring. Developing such a conception has several stages:

(A) Given the two-way ontological dependence noted above, we need to have a conception of the basic orientations humans need in order to be open to the world of ethics.

(B) We need to have some idea of the domain of the ethical: What region of reality is embraced by the *logos* of ethics?

(C) We need to have a conception of the nature of the evaluative that is sufficiently rich to do justice to the region of the ethical.

(D) We need to relate the evaluative so conceived to the deontic, and in general to reasons for action.

Turn now to (A). Mastery of the thick virtue and vice concepts is not just a matter of using them in speech (even psychopaths can do this to a degree by mastering rules),[7] but as Hume saw, it requires the fundamental emotional attunements of something he called the moral sense, along with its emotional conditions of possibility, notably benevolence (a desire for another's good) that is sufficiently extensive through sympathy.[8] For Hume, the openness of entities (people or actions) in their ethical mode of being (primarily as virtuous or vicious) is constituted by their "power" to excite the moral sense and its emotional conditions in this particular. Such a basic emotional orientation is not itself a concept but is a precondition of possessing properly ethical concepts. Ethics is not even intelligible to Hume's various moral monsters that are devoid of a moral sense, monsters such as his notorious psychopathic fictional individual who prefers to avoid the scratching of his little finger to the sufferings of untold millions. Armed only with "Reason" understood by Hume in a narrow sense as the operations of the *understanding*, a faculty abstracted from emotions and pleasure and pain, his eyes are not even opened to the worldhood of ethics.

However, the emotional openness to the world of ethics through something like the moral sense is not sufficient for ethical competence. For that we require familiarity[9] with a wide range of thick concepts such as hope, love, pride, joy, trust, honesty, courage, which in turn requires differing kinds of emotional construals[10] necessary for a grasp of appropriate expressions of pride and joy, when and how courage and honesty are called for, what is to be hoped for, whom to trust and when, and so on. For a highly developed account of what ethical openness requires we do not have to go back as far as Hume; perhaps the best source are the works of Iris Murdoch. Hume's moral sense is for Murdoch something much more active; Murdoch's "moral perception" is emotionally laden loving and just attention. That "perception" pervades the world as a whole, in its ethical aspect. For her, the work of interpreting the world to secure an *ethically* correct picture is pervasive, not just confined to discrete paradigmatically "moral" actions. It is not just confined to matters of obligation and duty, but incorporates the effortful interpretation and reinterpretation of people and situations continually (for ethical correctness is always *"beyond our full grasp"*—Broackes 2012, 64) through a vast range of thick concepts, not just those thought of as "moral" (whatever those are).[11]

To appreciate the range of thick concepts necessary for full openness to the world of ethics we need to turn to (B): the delineation of the region of the ethical. It is characteristic of the analytic tradition, and in particular writings on beneficence, to want to reduce the complexity of the moral or ethical terrain in at least three main ways: the unsituatedness of moral concepts (both in relation to context and to such things as culture and tradition (see, for example, the sparsely described examples that populate Parfit's work), the relative thinness of moral concepts (by contrast to the thick), and the paucity of moral notions; as Haidt (2013, 109) put it, "there is more to morality than harm and fairness." The relatively new area of social psychology called by those in the field "the science of morality" has proved an antidote to this tendency by directly asking people, away from artificial settings and thought experiments (such as trolley problems) how they think of morality in their everyday experience. By this means they have identified a number of ethical parameters within the following taxonomy (see Haidt 2013; Hofmann et al. 2014): Care/Harm; Fairness/Unfairness; Loyalty/ Disloyalty; Authority/Subversion; Sanctity/Degradation; Liberty/ Oppression; Honesty/Dishonesty; Self-Discipline/Lack of Self-Discipline. To this list I would add at least four more: Love/Hate, which as Hume (in book II of the *Treatise*) showed, are not the same as Benevolence/Malice, respectively; Creativity/Lack of Creativity; Hope/Despair; and Affability/Lack of Affability. Creativity as an aspect of the region of the ethical does justice to Kant's moral duty to cultivate one's talents and Nietzsche's ethical requirement to cultivate the "genius" within one. Affability speaks to our need for sociability in contexts of relaxation and problem solving (as long as the virtue is not confused with "niceness"), hope to our need to think of our projects as worthwhile in the context of our finitude, and so on.

What this shows is that the currency of value is a rather thin medium in which to think about ethics: in other work (2003, 2015b) I have suggested that in addition to value we should think in terms also of bonds (which speaks to loyalty, affability, and love), status (which speaks to authority, honesty, fairness, and sanctity), the good for an agent (which speaks to self-discipline and autonomy). I shall not elaborate on this pluralism of bases of ethical response[12] but shall instead outline a conception of the evaluative that does justice to the richness of the region of ethics identified under (A).

It is abundantly clear that to do justice to the region of ethics we need a large range of thick concepts that speak to various aspects of the region. Here are just a few examples: for Care/Benevolence we have generous, kind, sensitive, compassionate; for Harm we have cruel, malicious, mean, callous, reckless, negligent; for Love we have friendship, agape, tenderness, affection; for Fairness we have just, entitled, merited: for Unfairness (or distorted fairness) we have parasitism, what Nietzsche called "scientific fairness," and rigorous punitivism unleavened by mercy. For Disloyalty (or distorted loyalty) we have jingoism, blind loyalty; for Authority we have obedience (to, for instance, protocols, institutional rules, bosses' instructions); for Subversion we have authority complex, "playing God." For Self-discipline we have patience, cleanliness, industriousness, temperance, efficiency, nonprocrastination, and for Sanctity we may include many of the environmental virtues of respect for nature. Virtue notions associated with affability include Jane Austin's amiability, Aristotle's wittiness by contrast with boorishness and buffoonery, and Hume's cheerfulness by contrast with tendencies to "dissolute mirth."

This is but a small sample of some of the thick concepts that bear on some of the aspects of the region of the ethical. Nor do I intend to suggest rigidity here: the aspects of the ethical with their attendant thick concepts are fluid and interconnected. Further, many thick concepts provide links; for example, we can have the courage of someone resisting oppression or the courage of a journalist reporting unspeakably vicious harmful acts in highly dangerous places.

How do we understand the thick concepts, and what is their point? We turn now to (C): an explication of the nature of the evaluative sufficiently rich to do justice to the region of the ethical. That nature is understood through the thick concepts associated with the various aspects of that region. The point of such concepts is providing evaluative "shape" to situations, so that, as Dancy (1993, 112) puts it, their properties have a "practically related profile." Let us elaborate. According to Dancy, Debbie Roberts, and others, the thick concepts are "irreducibly thick"; that is, "evaluation and non-evaluation are deeply entangled in the content of thick concepts, and . . . the content of thick concepts cannot be disentangled into a thin evaluative component (or components) and a nonevaluative component" (Roberts 2011, 507). This is not to say that such concepts cannot have a rough nonevaluative characterization so we can have a basic idea of their domains of concern, but even this need not constitute a necessary condition for the proper application of a thick concept. For the thick concepts are nonevaluatively shapeless; that is, "there are no non-evaluative classifications corresponding to evaluative classifications" (Roberts 2011, 503). An illustration is provided by Little (2000, 279):

> The items grouped together under a moral classification such as "cruel" do not form a kind recognizable as such at the natural level . . . of the infinitely many ways of being cruel—kicking a dog, teasing a sensitive person, and forgetting to invite someone to a party might qualify—there is no saying what they have in common . . . except by helping oneself to the moral concept of cruelty.

An implication of this view according to Roberts is that the features in virtue of which acts are, for example, cruel or kind are dependent on context, and the nature of that dependence cannot be codified. In particular the features that make an act kind or honest in a context, for example, do not necessarily make that act right or good, even pro tanto.[13] This particularist position does not imply that ethics as such is uncodifiable in a suitably weak sense through what Hursthouse calls the v-rules, such as "Be kind" and "Be courageous."[14]

In providing shape to the nonevaluative (or richer shape to the less richly evaluative, such as benefiting) thick concepts denote evaluative properties that are "genuine features of the world" (Roberts

2013, 85). But how is the shape provided? Dancy (2013, 58) suggests that we should return to Williams's original account of thick concepts, concluding that "thick concepts are evaluative because competence with them requires a general understanding of their evaluative point, including the range of their practical relevance, the sorts of difference it can make that the concept is here instantiated." But how do we understand the idea of evaluative point? This understanding is provided at the most basic level by a grasp of what Haidt (2013) calls the "foundations" of the diverse aspects of the region of the ethical. We need to understand the varied roles such features as justice and loyalty play in human life as beings dwelling in a larger world. For example, the fairness/cheating foundation "evolved in response to the adaptive challenge of reaping the rewards of cooperation without getting exploited" (Haidt 2013, 178). The care/harm foundation "evolved in response to the adaptive challenge of caring for vulnerable children. It makes us sensitive to signs of suffering and need; it makes us despise cruelty" (Haidt 2013, 178). The loyalty/betrayal foundation evolved in response to the adaptive challenge of forming and maintaining coalitions. It makes us sensitive to signs that another person is (or is not) a team player (178). The authority/subversion foundation reflects our need for social hierarchy within institutions, and roles within those institutions. The love/hate foundation has as its biological basis an "attachment system" that "helps ensure that infants will feel and behave towards caregivers and love them in a way that enhances survival" (Peterson and Seligman 2004, 287) This feature of our natural endowment is with us throughout our lives (Peterson and Seligman 2004, 279). In other words, we are creatures that have a basic need for bonding with others.

The hope/despair foundation addresses a fundamental human need (without which we could not go on living, as Williams thinks) to think of our projects, creative endeavors, concerns, and loves as worthwhile, for which it is necessary to avoid existential despair, Heidegger's pervasive, totalizing boredom, and chronic severe depressive states.

The thick concepts associated with the various ethical foundations provide a more fine-grained shape to features located within those broad areas and thus enable a more nuanced understanding of the evaluative points of those features. For example, generosity, cruelty, callousness, indifference makes virtue/vice distinctions within the care/benevolence/harm nexus; tenderness, neglect, clinginess, passive aggression within the love/hate nexus; integrity, nonimitativeness, authenticity within the creativity/lack of creativity foundation.

We turn now to (D), the fourth aspect of delineating the *logos* of ethics. This is the link between the evaluative and reasons for action. What Dancy calls "practical relevance," as a general property of the thick concepts, denotes at least in part the functioning of thick concepts in our understanding of reasons for action. An act may be loyal or honest but not virtuously so. The loyal act may be an example of misguided loyalty; the honest act may be egregiously tactless. It is the virtuousness of an act that links evaluative shape to contributory reasons. An excellent example of the distinction between thick concepts as such and the properly virtue/vice concepts is provided by Karen Jones (2012) in her discussion of trustworthiness. She rightly objects to the "moralizing" of trustworthiness: it is not as such a virtue notion.[15] However, it is a thick concept that provides evaluative shape to the nonevaluative, and she gives an interesting account of this in terms of a general social need to be able to count on people. Our dependency in the form of a need to recruit others' agency involves expectations and responsiveness to such. But those of us who think that appropriate trust worthiness is a virtue need also to give an account of what features of trustworthiness in general make that kind of trustworthiness an *excellence* of character.

What counts as virtuously loyal, kind, honest, trustworthy links thick concept analysis to (some version of) virtue ethics. Virtuous kindness, trustworthiness, and so forth (whether in relation to character or acts) are thus theory-laden notions, dependent on one's virtue ethics. In the understanding of the virtuousness of actions there are significant differences among virtue ethicists. For some (notably Slote 2001) virtuousness depends on quality of motive; for others, such as Hursthouse (1999), virtuousness is understood in terms of the nature of or conformity to actions of virtuous agents acting characteristically; on my target-centered view (Swanton 2003, 2010, 2015a) the virtuousness of an act in respect of kindness, for example, depends on its meeting contextually relevant and salient aspects of the target(s) (what Aristotle calls the mean) of the virtue of kindness in relation to action. To know what constitutes hitting the (multidimensional) mean of a virtue we need to know the point and function of the virtue and the standards of virtue as a *satis* concept in relation to action[16], and that can be complex and contested. At a structural level we can at least say this: hitting the mean includes, for example (depending on such things as contextual salience and where the standards of virtuousness are set in relation to various forms of rightness), correctness in extent, time, motive, manner, instruments, in relation to that virtue.[17] This view I have developed elsewhere; here I merely point out that though a virtuous agent aims at the targets of the virtues, she may miss them through no fault of her own. Furthermore a nonvirtuous person may hit contextually relevant aspects of the target of relevant virtues, and thereby act rightly.

THE PARADOX OF SUPEREROGATION

A full defense of TCC requires consideration of many things, not only the metaphysics of TCC but also Williams's skeptical worries about the objectivity of ethics that properly deploys the thick concepts, and the relation between ethical and other modes of being, including the scientific broadly construed. Our defense of TCC is indirect, by putting TCC to work in resolving several paradoxes of beneficence—paradoxes that have their roots, I shall argue, in the twin evils of overly thin evaluative concepts and the construing of ethics through a framework of significance relations more suitable to the natural sciences.

We begin with the paradox of supererogation. The question here arises because we want to know whether philanthropy is supererogatory, and what it means to say that it is. Unfortunately answering these questions is not easy since the very definition of supererogation itself is far from clear. There are two problems. First, consider two nonequivalent definitions to be found in Dancy's (1993) *Moral Reasons,* which I quote:

(a) "Supererogatory acts . . . lie 'above and beyond the call of duty.'" (127)

(b) "The idea that some actions are supererogatory is just the idea that in certain circumstances agents may choose an action other than the one that would most promote the good." (167)

Let us begin with (b), which is the formulation of the supererogatory defended by Dancy. In relation to this definition, the paradox comes about in the following way. Assume what has been called the "good ought" tie-up. The tie-up apparently makes no room for superrerogation by virtue of:

1. We have most reason to produce the most good possible, and we ought to do what we have most reason to do.

The paradox occurs given the additional plausibility of:

2. In "certain circumstances agents may choose an action other than the one that would most promote the good." (Dancy 1993, 167)

Within consequentialist models of rationality (see the Simple Thought, the Hegemony of Promotion thesis, and the More Is Better Thesis cited above) (1) looks plausible. However in support of (2) is the view that the result is too demanding on the moral agent. Within his more general attack on consequentialism, Dancy supports (2), rejecting (1) as a truth of rationality and ethics. The evaluative here is understood in terms of agent-neutral value and the deontic in terms of reasons. Untying the "good-ought tie-up" occurs according to him when it is recognized that (1) applies to agent-neutral value only, but that sacrifice to the agent, generating agent-relative value, affects the balance of reasons in favor of actions.

Definition (b) of supererogation does not get to the heart of the problem of supererogation, namely that under the conception originally made famous by Urmson (1958), the paradox of supererogation affects both consequentialist and nonconsequentialist theories. As I argued in Swanton 2003, sacrifice of an extremely demanding sort can affect agent-relative considerations as well: the paradox of supererogation can apply as readily to love and care, as anyone who cares for her severely disabled child full time with little support can attest.

Let us turn, then, to definition (a) of supererogation, which allows for the recognition that the paradox of supererogation affects also versions of nonconsequentialism. Let us then reformulate the paradox as it applies to definition (a).

(1*) Where an action is a duty we have most reason to perform it, and we ought to do what we have most reason to do.

The paradox occurs given the additional plausibility of:

(2*) In certain circumstances agents may choose an action other than the one that would be a duty (under relevant conceptions of duty).

Within definition (a), however, there is a second serious unclarity, which directly affects beneficence and philanthropy. This involves the relation between supererogation and what Stangl (2016) calls "mundane" acts of, for example, generosity and charity. Citing Urmson, who claims, "It is possible to go just beyond one's duty by being a little more generous, forbearing, helpful . . . than *fair dealing demands*" (Stangl 2016, 358), she correctly argues that one must not confuse generosity and charity with duties of justice. It is a mistake to think that all acts of giving that are not required by "fair dealing" are over and above the call of duty: stingy acts of giving are prohibited by the virtue of generosity (Swanton 2015a: 44; Stangl 2016). It may still be claimed that all mundane acts of *generosity* are supererogatory (for by definition they are not stingy and thus prohibited), but this too is confusing. The general duty to be generous is not necessarily a duty to be generous to this person (or charity) here and now, but to call the realization of the general duty (what Kant calls a maxim) in such a case "over and above the call of duty" is seriously misleading. For one seems to be claiming that it is permissible not to perform any generous acts that are not mandated because they are over and above the call of duty, and thus permitted not to be generous at all except where a generous act is required. However, to act on that claim of permissibility is to violate Kant's duty of virtue of beneficence and the general requirement of virtue to be generous.

From now on, then, I shall reserve the notion of supererogation to describe admirable acts (such as the saintly and the heroic) that are over and beyond the call of duty.

Nonetheless on some views, such as Marcia Baron's (1995) Kant and Roger Crisp's (2013) Aristotle, the standards of duty of virtue as such make no room for supererogation, even for acts that are admirably saintly or heroic. Crisp (2013, 22) claims that for Aristotle it is clear that "the virtuous person's dying for others is not supererogatory; it is virtuous, and what is virtuous is a matter of doing one's duty. . . . Similarly with generosity. If the virtuous person makes large donations to Oxfam, for example, rather than spending the money on luxuries for himself, we can conclude it is his duty." For Crisp, Aristotle's "mean" at which a virtuous person aims is "a relation between circumstances and actions or feelings," and that mean is describable as "what is fitting or as one's duty" (22). So for Crisp we have a virtue-fittingness-duty tie-up, and thereby a virtue-ought tie-up. For him the paradox of supererogation (definition (a)) is resolvable by rejecting (2*), but this would be at the cost of an extremely demanding ethics.

Let us now deploy TCC to untie the virtue-duty-ought tie-up defended by Crisp. His anti-supererogationist stance puts too much weight on the thin concepts, in this case a thin conception of the link between Aristotle's conception of the mean, rightness (understood as correctness), duty, and fittingness. The correct action is understood in a way that is insensitive to the way the thick concepts work in relation to the mean. Or so I shall argue.

Certainly there is a virtue-fittingness tie-up, but it is not clear to me that there is a virtue-duty tie-up. Do all actions that conform to the mean involve duty? Cannot some actions conforming to the mean in action be fitting by being meritorious as opposed to being one's duty? On my view they can. The basis of the view that actions conforming to the mean can be meritorious but not required is that a virtue-based notion of fittingness is ambiguous. "Being fitting" can describe an act for which one has most reason in the sense that it is best in the circumstances relative to standards of admirable exemplars of virtue. On this view the fitting action is the best action where that is determined by the standards of admirable virtue. Let us assume that these standards are set by virtue understood as virtue possessed by some exemplar of saintliness or heroism, such as Jesus, Mandela, Gandhi, or the Homeric or Aristotelian warrior. Let us say that these exemplars possess admirable virtue, such as courage, love, or forgivingness (see Zagzebski 2010; Walker and Hennig 2004).

However, I shall argue that a fitting act could also describe an act performed for an undefeated reason, where one might have an undefeated reason to perform an act that is less than the best relative to such standards of admirability. Such acts may include acts of supererogation that one does not have a duty to perform even though they are admirable relative to the standards of admirable virtue and a duty relative to those standards.

The complexity introduced to the notions of fittingness and duty by the introduction of virtue notions is obscured by the description of supererogatory acts in terms of prosocial behavior such as volunteering, giving, and helping without subsuming such behavior under appropriate notions of virtue. When such relatively nonevaluative notions are used the Simple Thought seems to embody a rational requirement: Isn't it rational to give as much as possible, help as much as possible given that this will promote the most good? However, the ambiguity in the notion of fittingness introduced by virtue notions does not resolve the paradox. We still need to ask: Shouldn't *all* agents act according to duties set by standards of admirable virtue? It is not obvious that they should. Consider a self-improving agent aspiring to greater virtue or even admirable virtue. She may be, as Nietzsche puts it, "convalescent" or, as Annas (2011) puts it, an aspiring, learning agent. Should she always act according to admirable virtue? Nietzsche (1976, 4: "On the Higher Man" 13) suggests not; as he puts it in a warning, "Do not be virtuous beyond your strength!" There are two warnings here. First, the path to self-improvement is not smooth. In particular one should not directly emulate the most admirable exemplars on one's self-improving path, or at least not always. Second, as Nietzsche also points out, not all of us should even aspire to the most admirable virtue. Should all of us aspire to be "perfect," requiring us to "go and sell that thou hast, and give to the poor . . . and come and follow [Jesus]" (Matthew 19:16–21, KJV)? Certainly we should give to the poor, but should we all sell all that we have in doing this, and do the equivalent of following Jesus by living with the poorest, as do those belonging to some Christian charities, such as Servants? Such a demanding ethics is liable to result in or exhibit many serious failures of self-love, as in the cases of Farmer and Kravinsky (discussed in Angle 2009, 90–91).

We can now make sense of the paradoxical-looking (2*). "Duty of virtue" is ambiguous between duty according to admirable virtue, and duty where the bar is set lower according to a threshold conception, suitably calibrated according to the nature and development of the agent. The way this should be done is of course a highly complex issue, details of which cannot be explored further here.

THE PARADOX OF UNDERDETERMINATION

A classic problem in the ethics of beneficence and philanthropy is that of underdetermination by reason; for example, reason does not determine to whom one should give, how much, and to how many. Virtue ethics, it may be thought, is particularly vulnerable to the problem because virtue concepts such as generous and benevolent are vague and do not prescribe determinate action in all cases.

What more specifically is the problem? It is the paradox of underdetermination by reason caused by the following problem. It is generally considered rational to do what you have most reason to do. I understand "most reason" in the way it is understood by Ruth Chang (2009, 248): "You have most reason to choose x over y if the reasons for x outweigh, trump, silence, exclude, cancel, bracket or are more stringent than the reasons for y. Your choice of x is rationally determined." However, for many, including Chang, it is often the case that "the reasons for choice underdetermine what you should do" (248). You may have sufficient reason to choose either of two alternatives that may be incommensurable, or (on some understandings of tragic dilemmas) "your reasons may fail to deliver any justified choice whatsoever" (248).

It is often thought that when reasons for a specific choice "run out," you should simply plump for an alternative, but that seems unsatisfactory in the case of important life choices and important decisions like philanthropic giving. Here we seem faced with a dilemma, which is our second paradox of practical reason. Because we are justified in thinking that reasons have run out, further deliberation, even in important choices, seems inappropriate, but because plumping also seems inappropriate in such choices, continued deliberation about the merits of choices in search of what we have most reason to do seems appropriate.

Joseph Raz (2002, 47) appears to have offered a solution (in relation to the problem of incommensurability) by distinguishing between two conceptions of rationality:

> I will contrast two conceptions of human agency, which I will call the *rationalist* and the *classical*. In broad outline, the rationalist holds that paradigmatic human action is action taken because, of all the options open to the agent, it was, in the agent's view, supported by the strongest reason. The classical conception holds that the paradigmatic human action is one taken because, of all the options the agent considers rationally eligible, he chooses to perform it.

He prefers the classical conception—one according to which it may be rational to choose something even if there is not most reason to perform it, even in Chang's sense—concluding:

> The classical conception of human agency with its reliance on widespread incommensurabilities gains support from ordinary human experience, which teaches us that quite commonly people do not survey all the options open to them before choosing what to do. Rather, they find an option that they believe not to be excluded by reason and that appeals to them and pursue it. (Raz 2002, 65)

But could not the way you choose what "appeals" be criticizable? What if you are pusillanimous, vacillating, hugely anguished because your choice is not rationally determined? Or could you not be criticizable for giving up too soon in the survey of options? Chang's own solution is to look for a feature not itself normatively assessed (an act of creation) that rationalizes a choice even where reasons have run out. We create a reason by an act of will. We "take" a reason to confer normativity and resolve the deadlock, thus creating a reason where none existed before. These are voluntarist reasons. But could not your act of will also be criticizable?

Again the problem arises because the crucial concepts deployed— will, choice, appeal, plumping—are too thin; they are not concepts suitable to the *logos* of ethics. The virtue ethical solution to this paradox outlined below does not have this difficulty for it supplies standards for so-called plumping where reasons have run out. Plumping, an apparently descriptive feature, can be normatively assessed by standards of virtue. Let us investigate those virtue-based standards. Consider a case of career choice related to philanthropy. You have been offered a very good position in an aid agency but at the same time have a chance to do a further degree in politics, economics, and philosophy at Oxford. You are tempted by the academic route, but you also realize that your knowledge of the world relevant to working for aid organizations will be enhanced by your Oxford studies. After much deliberation you find that reasons have run out. At a party you talk to a well-known figure in aid, Jones. No further reasons are given that you had not already considered: rather, fired with enthusiasm, you choose the aid agency. But things could have been different. You do not meet Jones, but an academic friend alerts you to a scholarship at Oxford. You apply and are successful. You choose Oxford. What we have described here are two different narratives. You have gone along with the narrative flow of your life: Jones talks to you, or, on the alternative scenario, your academic friend alerts you to an opportunity. Life has taken you down a certain path. This does not constitute a reason for acting that breaks the tie between reasons.

But is there not something arbitrary about this? Is this any better than "mere" plumping? If what you have done is within the context of the narrative direction of your life, much of which is not within your control, going along with that direction can conform to narrative virtue or not. Such conforming to virtue need not be a matter of excellence in (further) deliberation. How so? What is narrative virtue, and what are the thick concepts that are relevant here? Consider our narrative again, but with this difference: Jones talks to you, but you are an obsessive deliberator unable to make up your mind. You prevaricate. You lack confidence in people and yourself. You cannot take the plunge and commit to the aid agency. We have here narrative vices: tendencies to obsessively deliberate when, as far as you can see, reasons have run out; tendencies to demand/want to be in full control of your own destiny; a disposition to vacillate and/or prevaricate; unwillingness to commit; lack of courage and confidence in the future—a lack of a virtue of hope. Failure to be fired up by Jones's encouragement may manifest all or some of these vices. Alternatively you may manifest opposite vices: you are the sort who imagines reasons have run out when they have not; maybe you are intellectually lazy, maybe you are so fearful of the future you cannot bear to think about it. Maybe you are the sort who is excessively suggestible; the moment someone makes a half-decent suggestion you go along with it. Maybe you want others to control your life. Where your plumping for the aid agency job conforms to narrative virtue your choice is fitting, even where it is underdetermined by reason. It is fitting since it conforms to virtue or at least does not manifest vice, even though your choice of the job over the degree is not made *for* an undefeated reason but is rather the result of an enthusiastic response to Jones's conversation. You have gone with the narrative flow but in a way that is fitting.

Let us say a little more about narrative virtue. A core virtue of rationality broadly specified, namely a disposition to be responsive to reasons is, as we might put it, narratively differentiated; that is, it is manifested within the context of the narrative features of your life. It includes in its differentiated form a disposition to stop the search for what one has most reason to do where appropriate, and to go with the narrative flow, provided that is fitting. That in turn is determined by conformity to a complex range of narrative differentiations of the broad virtue of responsiveness to reasons, only some of which are mentioned above.

Finally, notice what narrative virtue does not demand. It does not demand that quite independently of your life story, your interests, your traits, you should choose a career that is optimific on the grand scale, for example one that maximizes your chances of being philanthropic in a grand sense, or an aid worker saving lives.

Let us now apply this analysis to reasons of philanthropy, such as choosing a charity. If the narrative particularities of your life feature in your choice where there is underdetermination by reason, can they not also feature in your choice of charity even where your choice produces less overall good than other choices? Certainly there may be much incommensurability, but is it permissible to knowingly give in a suboptimific way? Attention to evaluative features highlighted by the thick concepts, appropriate to the several foundations of ethics, shows how such giving can be virtuous. The bonds of love and loyalty, the bonds to self that drive prudence, are legitimate moral forces within a narrative context, attesting not just to the psychology of such giving but also to its virtuousness. The expression of love, solidarity, gratitude to a loved one or to one's community or to an institution such as your local Cancer Society, which has provided you free of charge desperately needed psychological services, may legitimately determine choice of charitable endeavor.

Gratitude, loyalty, solidarity, caring are all virtues legitimizing such charity.

THE "IT MAKES NO DIFFERENCE" PARADOX

The paradox of "It makes no difference" concerns the requirement to do what we apparently have no reason to do. In these cases people may collectively aim to provide a good or solve a problem. Such a good cannot be provided through individual action or as effectively provided through individual action. Let us say that collective action to provide the good is realizable; the collective aim is agreed upon, as well as the method for obtaining it. Yet it turns out that it is true of each individual contribution required to secure the good that that contribution makes no difference to the securing of the outcome. Technically this paradox is not quite the same as the problem of charitable donations being a "drop in the ocean," but the thick virtue concepts can be applied to that problem too.

In general the No Difference Problem can be described thus: It makes no difference whether or not I make my contribution, avoid paying, pick this flower, dig up this bulb, and so on; so I have no reason to make this contribution, refrain from picking this flower, and so on. It will be my argument that there can be such a reason, a reason under a suitable virtue description. Nefsky (2015) claims there are two approaches to resolving the paradox. The first is to deny that in paradigm cases of the problem the description of the case as one where the act "makes no difference" is false. The second, of which my solution is a version, "rejects the implication from 'it makes no difference' to there is 'no reason to do it'" (246). My version is one where the reasons are described at a fundamental level through the thick virtue/vice concepts. Call this version the Thick Concept Solution.

This solution has three main parts. In a relevant case the following is true:

(a) The action of not A'ing is subsumed under a relevant vice concept, such as "parasitical," "unfair" "mean," "callous."

(b) Insofar as the action of not A'ing is, for example, *parasitical*, that constitutes a reason not to do it.

(c) That reason is ultimate or basic in that being parasitical is not trumped by a reason specified in a descriptive way, such as my contribution, payment, and so forth does not make a perceptible difference; my contribution does not constitute a share. That is to say we cannot say either that failure to A ceases to be parasitical or unfair because it makes no difference, or that my failure to A's being parasitical or unfair ceases to have negative valence just because my A'ing makes no difference.

The Thick Concept Solution has been taken in relation to the virtue concept of fairness by Garrett Cullity (2000, 22). He makes an analogy between the "imperceptibilist," she who claims that she has no reason to make a contribution since it would make no perceptible difference, and the free-rider:

In the same way that the free rider arrogates special privileges to himself, the imperceptibilist is arrogating special privileges to herself. In circumstances in which there is a collective imperative that we ought to be meeting, she is leaving it to others to meet it, without being prepared to do it herself, and without any justification for treating herself differently from them.

Both are acting in a way that is unfair.

Fairness, however, is not the only thick concept used to specify reasons in Making No Difference cases. Rather that concept is apt for only some kinds of cases of Making No Difference. Can we provide more structure to the Thick Concepts Solution? The most general virtue that can be deployed to supply reasons for actions that "make no difference" is a nameless virtue whose field or domain of concern is doing your share or "doing your bit." Three things need to be noted about the application of this virtue we call (being disposed to) "doing your share." First, not all cases of actions that individually make no difference to the production of a collective good but that collectively would cause a significant benefit would count as failure to do one's share were the action to be omitted. Nefsky (2015, 246) gives the following example: "While large scale consumer patterns can have a major impact on the lives of people across the globe, it's hard to imagine that a single purchase would make a difference." Buying a dozen eggs or a cake at a café can hardly count as not doing one's share to mitigate the harms of consumerism. Contrast the vagueness, open-endedness, and indefiniteness of the "problem of consumerism" with the closed system described by Parfit's (1984, 76) "drops of water" case (adapted by Nefsky 2015, 247). The collective good is saving a specified number of people (ten thousand) dying of thirst in the desert, a good that would be secured if the same number of people contributed a pint each to a water cart, the contents of which are to be distributed equally. But one such individual contribution is not enough to make a difference. Yet surely individual failure to contribute your pint would count as not doing your share.

Second, not all cases of not doing one's share count as acting contrary to the *virtue* of doing one's share. What counts as an excellence in the field of doing one's share is highly complex. Having and manifesting the virtue is compatible with appropriately not doing one's share in specified circumstances, just as excellence in a disposition to honesty is compatible with appropriately lying on certain occasions. For example, there may be cases of failing to help or contribute when arrogating special privileges to yourself is fair and justified. This is true in Nefsky's (2015, 257) Small case, where "Small" "is an adult trapped in a two-year-old's body" and will make no difference to pushing a car up a hill. Even though both in "drops of water" (Parfit 1984, 76) and "Small" contributions make no perceptible difference, in "drops of water" the failure to contribute falls under a vice concept, whereas Small's failure to contribute does not. Here is another example: My failure to vote when my vote makes no difference is something that in New Zealand I have a right to do, and I may be exercising that right for good reason. I like none of the options, and I do not prefer any of the evils on offer to the other evils. No vice term, such as laziness, apathy, and so forth, need be applicable.

Third, the general vice of "not doing one's bit" can in different contexts be given different descriptions, for example being callous, negligent, mean, and parasitical. My failure to make a contribution for a collective good that, when taken on its own, makes no difference can be parasitical, unfair, self-indulgent, or callous, depending on the circumstances. Cullity (2000) analogizes the unfairness of my failure to make a contribution to the parasitism of the free-rider. My collecting just a few bluebells for my garden from a large bluebell wood near Reading is mean when I can easily afford to buy the same number at a nursery; my picking a small bunch of daffodils (in different spots) in Hagley Park Christchurch because I find them attractive and want to have some for myself is self-indulgent and selfish. My contributing in an imperceptible way to the torture of an individual in Parfit's (1984, 80) fictional case, where each individual makes no perceptible difference to the eventual "torture" of the victim, is describable as callous, where the case is filled out in ways that make the application of that term appropriate.[18] Where the case is underdescribed, as so often happens, we cannot be sure of the correct application of a relevant thick concept; the point is, however, that it is not sufficient to properly withhold a vice term to a person's act just because that act "makes no difference." To describe the reasons in Making No Difference cases without use of thick concepts renders invisible important evaluative properties of one's acts and omissions.

However, the existence of a general virtue of doing one's share, which can be applicable even in Making No Difference cases, is apparently denied by Nefsky. She claims that the Thick Concept Solution, such as Cullity's, that relies on (putatively) relevant features other than the difference you make does not work. For it still remains true that if your act won't make a difference it cannot constitute a share in a context of participation in the production of a collective good. This is precisely because the putative share to the collective good makes no difference. We are driven back to specifying the ultimate reason for acting in terms of a causal framework, and within this framework Nefsky's point seems undeniable: my contribution taken on its own causes no increase in the good sought. My "share" is no share, so how can I have a reason to contribute?

The Thick Concept Solution relies on the idea that the causal *logos* of making no difference as such is the wrong *logos* for specifying reasons. The *logos* of the ethical is the *logos* of thick concepts. In a solution such as Cullity's we rely on subsuming the action that makes no difference under a thick concept (fairness) where fairness has a resultance base that is shapeless. Mastery of that concept involves knowledge of the evaluative point of justice; applying that concept in a competent way involves understanding when and when not failure to contribute is or is not parasitical, when and when not resentment at putative unfairness exhibits a resentment-filled dog-in-the-manger attitude (see Glover 1975, 182), when and when not one's contribution would exhibit a problematic self-sacrificing attitude, and so on.

What makes something fair and so forth cannot be captured within a "scientific," merely causal *logos* where it is my making a *perceptible* contribution that amounts to a share, and under that description of the reason it turns out to be no reason at all. But here lies the mistake. The reasons salient and basic in the *logos* of practical reality are not like this; they are the virtue/vice reasons. Furthermore, with competence with the thick concepts describing such reasons in hand, these features enable us to distinguish nonvicious from vicious cases of failing to act in Making No Difference cases. In many cases, of course, whether or not failures to act in No Difference cases are nonvirtuous is controversial. Many are relatively demanding actions or omissions that require large-scale compliance to achieve the collective good.

Virtue ethics, based on Thick Concept Centralism and by contrast with forms of welfarism, has not been a traditional approach to the philosophy of beneficence. Thick Concept Centralism, the foundation of virtue ethics, needs to be taken more seriously as a metaphysically respectable approach to ethics in general, and one that is capable not only of providing a more nuanced approach to philanthropy but of resolving paradoxes of rationality related to beneficence in general.[19]

NOTES

1. This is Philippa Foot's (1985, 198) term.
2. It is important to note that I am not talking specifically about "moral" reasons here, a notion that does not have a natural home in virtue ethics. Not only

is that notion extremely narrow in the analytic tradition, but it is also highly contested as a taxonomic category within the practical domain. On this issue see Swanton 2014.

3. Notice that this view does not imply that the thick is prior to the thin: "The specific and the general concepts may be interdependent" (Hurley 1989, 14).

4. Cited from *Aristoteles Metaphysics IX* by Golob, *Heidegger on Concepts*, 82. See also Heidegger 1982, 205ff. Compare Gadamer (1989, 412): "Thus the relational ordering that is logos is much more than the mere correspondence of words and things. . . . The truth contained in the logos is not that of mere perception (of noein), nor just letting being appear; rather, it always places being in a relationship, assigning something to it."

5. Heidegger, *Logik: Die Frage nach der Wahrheit* (1976), 153, cited in Golob 2014, 72. See Golob for excellent discussion of the "a as b" structure in Heidegger, and his insistence that "a as b" cannot "be identified with an inchoate or inexplicit propositional or judgmental intentionality" (73).

6. Although aspects of "the four-fold unitary openness" are separately described for the purposes of understanding them, they are not separate *in re*. Explicit discussion of the other aspects of the fourfold is beyond the scope of this chapter, but see Swanton 2013.

7. See Bloom (2013: 33–40) on the emotional deficits of psychopaths by contrast with their knowledge of right and wrong in relation to rules.

8. For a detailed account of Hume's views see Swanton 2015c.

9. The idea of familiarity is operationalized in social-cognitive psychology, through the notion of accessibility and related concepts. Briefly, the "more frequently a construct is activated, or the more recently it is primed, the more accessible it should be for processing social information. . . . Frequently activated constructs, over time, should be more easily or 'chronically' accessible" (Lapsley and Narvaez 2005, 29). Familiarity with the *logos* of ethics requires familiarity with a vast range of thick evaluative concepts and related notions of excellence, so that ethical categories become "salient, chronically accessible, easily primed, and readily utilized" (31).

10. For the idea of emotional construal see Roberts 2003.

11. For an appreciation of this aspect of Murdoch's thought see Taylor 1996.

12. For elaboration see Swanton 2015b.

13. There may be some exceptions to this claim in the case of some thick concepts such as cruel or just. See further on "radical particularism" and its relationship to the thick concepts Dancy 2004.

14. I defend such a version of codifiability compatible with Dancy-style particularism in Swanton 2015a.

15. We should go further: thick concepts need not even have as part of their meaning a pro or con evaluation, even pro tanto; they need not be either honorific or pejorative independent of context. Dancy (2013, 58) gives the example of lewd; I offer a more genteel example, sentimental.

16. By that is meant that to be virtuous is to be virtuous enough: one needs to meet a threshold of virtue on which one can improve.

17. For an interesting case consider Slote's example of prosecuting out of malice discussed by Sverdlik (2011, chapter 7). For Sverdlik, if the prosecutor's motives are mixed and he "does things by the book," then the malicious motive does not affect the deontic nature of the act. I concur. He does the right thing for the wrong reasons. The case is rather like Kant's honest but not well-motivated shopkeeper. On the other hand, in a context of justice, if the malicious prosecutor driven by maliciousness "cuts corners," he has the wrong motive and deploys wrong instruments; we may be more willing to say his prosecuting was wrong even if the verdict itself were correct. Given combinatorial and degree vagueness concerning the contextual salience of dimensions of the mean and what it takes to hit targets on any dimension, there need not be a truth of the matter here (see Swanton 2010).

18. Thanks to Garrett Cullity here.

19. May I express my gratitude to the University of Austin for an invitation to present at the Royal Conference on Philanthropy, and to the audience at that conference; my thanks also to Garrett Cullity for comments; and also to the audience at the Australasian Association of Philosophy Conference, Canberra, July 2014, including Dirk Baltzy, Daniel Star, Garrett Cullity, and Monique Jonas, whose comments and questions led to improvement on an early draft. I am also very grateful to excellent editorial advice from Paul Woodruff.

REFERENCES

Angle, Steven C. (2009). *Sagehood: The Contemporary Significance of Neo-Confucian Philosophy*. Oxford: Oxford University Press.

Annas, Julia. 2011. *Intelligent Virtue*. Oxford: Oxford University Press.

Anscombe, G. E. M. 1958 "Modern Moral Philosophy." Reprinted (1997) in Roger Crisp and Michael Slote (eds.), *Virtue Ethics*. Oxford: Oxford University Press, 26–44.

Baron, Marcia (1995). *Kantian Ethics Almost without Apology*. Ithaca, NY: Cornell University Press.

Bloom, Paul (2013). *The Origins of Good and Evil*. New York: Crown.

Broackes, Justin (2012). Introduction in Justin Broackes (ed.), *Iris Murdoch, Philosopher: A Collection of Essays*. Oxford: Oxford University Press, 1–92.

Chang, Ruth (2009). "Voluntarist Reasons and the Sources of Normativity." In David Sobel and Steven Wall (eds.), *Reasons for Action*. Cambridge, UK: Cambridge University Press, 243–271.

Crisp, Roger (2013). "Supererogation and Virtue." In Mark Timmons (ed.), *Normative Ethics*, vol. 3. Oxford: Oxford University Press, 13–34.

Cullity, Garrett (2000). "Pooled Beneficence." In Michael J. Almeida (ed.), *Imperceptible Harms and Benefits*. Dordrecht: Kluwer, 9–42.

Dancy, Jonathan (1993). *Moral Reasons*. Oxford: Blackwell.

Dancy, Jonathan (2004). *Ethics without Principles*. Oxford: Clarendon Press.

Dancy, Jonathan (2013). "Practical Concepts." In Simon Kirchin (ed.), *Thick Concepts*. Oxford: Oxford University Press, 44–59.

Foot, Philippa (1985). "Utilitarianism and the Virtues." *Mind* 94 (374): 196–209.

Gadamer, Hans-Georg (1989). *Truth and Method*. Translated by Joel Weinsheimer and Donald G. Marshall. 2d edition. New York: Crossroad.

Glover, Jonathan and M. J. Scott-Taggart (1975). "It Makes No Difference Whether or Not I Do It." *Proceedings of the Aristotelian Society, Supplementary Volumes* 49: 171–209.

Golob, Sacha. (2014). *Heidegger on Concepts, Freedom and Normativity*. Cambridge: Cambridge University Press.

Haidt, Jonathan (2013). *The Righteous Mind: Why Good People Are Divided by Politics and Religion*. London: Penguin Books.

Heidegger, Martin (1982). *Basic Problems of Phenomenology*. Translated by Albert Hofstadter. Revised edition. Bloomington: Indiana University Press.

Heidegger, Martin (1994). *Basic Questions of Philosophy*. Translated by Richard Rojcewicz and Andre Schuwer. Bloomington: Indiana University Press.

Heidegger, Martin (1995). *The Fundamental Concepts of Metaphysics*. Translated by W. McNeill and N. Walker. Bloomington: Indiana University Press.

Hofmann, Wilhelm, Daniel C. Wisnieski, Mark J. Brandt, and Linda J. Skitka (2014). "Morality in Everyday Life." *Science* 345 (6202): 1340–1343.

Hurley, S. L. 1989. *Natural Reasons: Personality and Polity*. New York: Oxford University Press.

Hurley, Susan (1985). "Objectivity and Disagreement." In Ted Honderich (ed.), *Morality and Objectivity: A Tribute to J. L. Mackie*. New York: Routledge, 54–97.

Hursthouse, Rosalind (1999). *On Virtue Ethics*. Oxford: Oxford University Press.

Jones, Karen (2012). "Trustworthiness." *Ethics* 123 (1): 61–85.

Lapsley, Daniel K. and Darcia Narvaez (2005). "Moral Psychology at the Crossroads." In Daniel K. Lapsley and F. Clark Power (eds.), *Character Psychology and Character Education*. Notre Dame, IN: University of Notre Dame Press, 18–35.

Little, Margaret Olivia (2000). "Moral Generalities Revisited." In Brad Hooker and Margaret Olivia Little (eds.), *Moral Particularism*. Oxford: Clarendon Press, 276–304.

McDowell, John (1994). *Mind and World*. Cambridge, MA: Harvard University Press.

McDowell, John (1995). "Two Sorts of Naturalism." In Rosalind Hursthouse, Gavin Lawrence, and Warren Quinn (eds.), *Virtues and Reasons: Philippa Foot and Moral Theory*. Oxford: Clarendon Press, 149–179.

McDowell, John (2007). "What Myth?" *Inquiry* 50 (4): 338–351.

Nefsky, Julia (2015). "Fairness, Participation and Collective Harm." In Mark Timmons (ed.), *Oxford Studies in Normative Ethics*, vol. 5. Oxford: Oxford University Press, 245–271.

Nietzsche, Friedrich (1976). "Thus Spoke Zarathustra." In Walter Kaufmann (ed. and trans), *The Portable Nietzsche*. New York: Penguin, 103–439.Parfit, Derek (1984). *Reasons and Persons*. Oxford: Oxford University Press.

Peterson, Christopher and Martin E. P. Seligman (2004). *Character Strengths and Virtues: A Handbook and Classification*. Cary, NC: Oxford University Press.

Raz, Joseph (2002). *Engaging Reason: On the Theory of Value and Action*. Oxford: Oxford University Press.

Roberts, Debbie (2011). "Shapelessness and the Thick." *Ethics* 121 (3): 489–520.

Roberts, Debbie (2013). "It's Evaluation, Only Thicker." In Simon Kirchin (ed.), *Thick Concepts*. Oxford: Oxford University Press, 78–96.

Roberts, Robert C. (2003). *Emotions: An Essay in Aid of Moral Psychology*. Cambridge, UK: Cambridge University Press.

Slote, Michael (2001). *Morals from Motives*. Oxford: Oxford University Press.

Stangl, Rebecca (2016). "Neo-Aristotelian Supererogation." *Ethics* 126 (2): 339–365.

Sverdlik, Steven (2011). *Motive and Rightness*. Oxford: Oxford University Press.

Swanton, Christine (2003). *Virtue Ethics: A Pluralistic View*. Oxford: Oxford University Press.

Swanton, Christine (2010). "Virtue Ethics and the Problem of Moral Disagreement." *Philosophical Topics* 38 (2), 157–180.

Swanton, Christine (2014). "The Notion of the Moral: The Relation between Virtue Ethics and Virtue Epistemology." *Philosophical Studies* 171 (1): 121–134.

Swanton, Christine (2015a). "A Particularist but Codifiable Virtue Ethics." In Mark Timmons (ed.) *Normative Ethics*, vol. 5. Oxford: Oxford University Press, 38–63.

Swanton, Christine (2015b). "Pluralistic Virtue Ethics." In Lorraine Besser-Jones and Michael Slote (eds.), *The Routledge Companion to Virtue Ethics*. New York: Routledge, 209–221.

Swanton, Christine (2015c). *The Virtue Ethics of Hume and Nietzsche*. New York: Wiley-Blackwell.

Taylor, Charles (1996). "Iris Murdoch and Moral Philosophy." In Maria Antonaccio and William Schweiker (eds.), *Iris Murdoch and the Search for Human Goodness*. Chicago: University of Chicago Press, 3–28.

Thomas, Alan (2006). "Consequentialism, Integrity, and Demandingness." In Timothy Chappell (ed.), *The Problem of Moral Demandingness: New Philosophical Essays*. London: Palgrave Macmillan, 123–147.

Urmson, J. O. (1958). "Saints and Heroes." In A. I. Melden (ed.), *Essays on Moral Philosophy*. Seattle: University of Washington Press, 198–216.

Walker, Lawrence and Karl Hennig (2004). "Differing Conceptions of Moral Exemplarity: Just Brave and Caring." *Journal of Personality and Social Psychology* 93, 845–860.

Wall, John (2005). *Moral Creativity: Paul Ricoeur and the Poetics of Possibility.* Oxford: Oxford University Press.

Williams, Bernard (1985). *Ethics and the Limits of Philosophy.* London: Fontana.

Williams, Bernard (1995). "What Does Intuitionism Imply?" In *Making Sense of Humanity and Other Philosophical Papers.* Cambridge, UK: Cambridge University Press, 182–191.

Zagzebski, Linda (2010). "Exemplarist Virtue Theory." In Heather Battaly (ed.), *Virtue and Vice: Moral and Epistemic.* New York: Wiley-Blackwell, 39–55.

Chapter 3

Doing Good and Doing the Best

JEFF MCMAHAN

LESS EFFECTIVE ALTRUISM

When Leona Helmsley, a rather unpleasant American plutocrat, died in 2008, the estimated value of the estate she left was between $3 billion and $8 billion. She bequeathed a tiny fraction of this to certain relatives, pointedly omitting others. She also left $12 million to her dog, an amount that was subsequently reduced to $2 million by the trustees of the estate. The remainder of the fortune went to the Helmsley Charitable Trust. The mission statement of the Charitable Trust stipulated that the money should be used, first, for "purposes related to the provision of care for dogs" and, second, for "such other charitable activities as the Trustee shall determine." The mission statement had earlier listed a third aim—"provision of medical and health care for indigent people, with emphasis on providing care to children"—but Helmsley later deleted that clause (Toobin 2008, 41).

After her death, I was briefly interviewed over the telephone for an article on the legal challenges to her bequest. I was asked whether Helmsley acted impermissibly in leaving her money to dogs rather than to people. My response was rather simplistic and naive. I said:

> To give even two million dollars to a single little dog is like setting the money on fire in front of a group of poor people. To bestow that amount of money is contemptuous of the poor, and that may be one reason she did it. But to give such a large sum of money to dogs generally is not frivolous. I think it shows some misplaced priorities, but many bequests do. In a world where there is starvation and poverty, you can say that it's wrong to give money to universities, or museums, or, worst of all, to divide it up for your children and heirs who are already rich. Welfare for dogs is better than more pampering of the rich. It may indicate misplaced priorities, but it [is] not frivolous or silly. It [the bequest "for the care of dogs"] is disgraced by the context, but the two bequests should be separately evaluated. (quoted in Toobin 2008, 47)

Among the thoughts I had when I made this comment was that a major activity of charities that care for dogs is finding homes for strays that would otherwise either be "euthanized" or left to live by scavenging, often in a diseased or injured condition, only to be eventually killed beneath the wheels of a car. Preventing a vast number of dogs from suffering one or the other of these fates seemed to me a justifiable and even worthy use of this woman's money.

But of course Helmsley's billions could have been used instead to prevent human suffering and to save the lives of a very large number of people. So the relevant issue was essentially comparative: not whether preventing canine suffering and saving the lives of dogs was a *good* use of the money, but whether using the money for those purposes was morally acceptable when it was possible to use it in ways that would have done much more good. The Helmsley bequest thus raises the more general question whether it can be morally permissible to donate money to one charitable cause when one could instead donate the money in a different way that would prevent more suffering or provide greater benefits.

Most people assume that the money Helmsley controlled at the time of her death was hers to dispose of as she wished. If she had really wanted, for example, to convert it to cash and burn it in a latter-day bonfire of the vanities, even outside a shelter for the homeless, that would, many people assume, have been her right. Although I cannot argue against it here, I think that this view is mistaken. Not only would she not have had a liberty-right or permission to destroy the money, but she would also not have had a "right to do wrong"—that is, a claim-right or right against interference if she had attempted to destroy the money. Helmsley had legal rights to more resources than it could have been morally justifiable for her to own, possess, or control. Most of her money, in my view, was legally but not morally hers to dispose of. That which she was not morally entitled to retain, she was morally required to give away. But because she had no moral entitlement to that which she was required to give away, her wishes in the matter of its disposal were morally irrelevant. It is arguable that the portion of her wealth to which she had a legal but not a moral title belonged to no one and ought to have been used in a way that would have done the most good, impartially considered. When there are resources to which no one has a claim, the default assumption is that they ought to be used to do the most good, taking into account that this may involve giving some priority to those who are worst off.

But some of the money that legally belonged to Helmsley at the time of her death was also morally hers to control. Let us assume that she was morally entitled to leave that money to wealthy relatives or even to gather it while she was on her deathbed and burn it in her fireplace. In that case it would have been genuinely supererogatory for her to give it instead to organizations that would use it to provide care for dogs. Some philosophers think, however, that even when it is supererogatory to give money to a charity, once one has decided to give a certain amount, one ought to give it in a way that would do more rather than less good (e.g., Pummer 2016 and Horton 2017). These philosophers acknowledge, of course, that there are limits to the amount of effort one must devote to determining which charity would be most effective, but they do insist that, given the information that one can be reasonably expected to acquire, one must give the money in the way that would do the most good.

A CONDITIONAL REQUIREMENT TO DO THE BEST

This view is, however, rather puzzling. One may wonder how, if it is permissible not to give at all, it could be impermissible to give to a less effective rather than to a more effective charity. Most people believe that not only *whether* to give to charity but also *to which* charity to give is entirely discretionary. When it is morally permissible not to give to charity at all, it is also permissible, most people believe, to give to whichever charity one prefers, for whatever reason. It is generally believed, for example, that it is permissible to give to a charity that supports efforts to discover a cure for a rare and not terribly debilitating disease rather than to one that seeks a cure for a common and devastating disease. Indeed, many believe that it is no less laudable to give to the first than to give to the second.

Yet there do seem to be instances in which it is supererogatory to benefit another—that is, it is permissible not to provide any benefit—but in which one is morally required to provide the greater benefit if one provides any benefit at all. Derek Parfit (1982, 131) has presented one such case. "Suppose," he writes, "that I have three alternatives":

A: at some great cost to myself, saving a stranger's right arm;

B: doing nothing;

C: at the same cost to myself, saving both the arms of this stranger.

Parfit claims that, although the cost to the agent of either of the two acts of rescue may make it permissible for him to do neither, once he accepts the cost of saving one arm, it becomes impermissible for him not to save the other. That is, while it is permissible to save *neither* arm, it is not permissible to save *only one* arm.

One might think that instances of charitable giving, such as the Helmsley bequest, are relevantly like this case of Parfit's. For both in Parfit's case and in cases in which charitable giving is supererogatory, the agent can choose between doing less good and doing more good at an equivalent personal cost. And one might thus infer that, because the agent in Parfit's case is morally required to bestow the greater benefit, the same must be true in cases of charitable giving.

But in fact Parfit's case differs from ordinary instances of supererogatory charitable giving in at least two relevant respects. First, once the agent in Parfit's case has ruled out the option of doing nothing, he can either confer only one benefit at great cost to himself or confer that *same* benefit to the same person *and* confer *another* equally great benefit at no further personal cost. While this agent had sufficient reason to provide neither benefit, he has *no* reason to provide only one rather than both. To prevent the loss of only one of the stranger's arms would be *gratuitously* to allow the stranger to suffer the loss of an arm. And to allow a great harm to occur when one could prevent it at no cost to anyone is wrong.

By contrast, if Helmsley had chosen to leave her wealth to charities that would have produced greater good by benefiting persons rather than dogs, she would not have produced the same benefits she in fact produced together with others. Rather, if she had given to more effective charities, that would have been worse for the beneficiaries of her actual bequest. For Helmsley's action to have been relevantly like that of the agent in Parfit's case, she would have had to benefit only dogs rather than providing the same benefits to the same dogs while also benefiting people at no additional cost. In general, when one gives to a less effective charity, one does not gratuitously fail to benefit those who would have benefited, and by more, if one had given to a more effective charity. Each charitable option would have victims in the sense that each would be worse for those who would have benefited from a different option. The failure to benefit any potential beneficiary is not gratuitous because it enables someone else to be benefited instead, even if to a lesser degree.

A second way in which Parfit's case differs from ordinary charitable giving is that, as the case is presented, there is no reason why the agent might prefer to save only one arm rather than both, whereas people often have reasons for preferring to give to a less effective rather than a more effective charity. Helmsley, for example, like many good people who volunteer to work at animal shelters, cared specially about dogs. It was important to her to provide care for dogs who would otherwise have been killed or suffered miserable lives. There would therefore have been a cost *to her* in forgoing the option of helping dogs. Because of this, the overall cost to her of using her money to save people would have been greater than the cost to her of using the same amount of money to save dogs.

In summary, in Parfit's case, doing more good rather than (or, more precisely, in addition to) less good has no cost for the agent and is better rather than worse for the beneficiary of the lesser benefit. But in the Helmsley case, giving a fixed sum to charities that would do more good would have been worse both for her and for those who benefited from her gift to charities that did less good.

The same is true of charitable giving generally. Most choices between preventing greater harm by giving to a more effective charity and preventing less harm by giving to a less effective charity are like Helmsley's choice rather than the choice that the agent in Parfit's case faces. People often give to a less effective charity because they have some personal reason for caring about the work of that particular charity, and their failure to prevent more harm is not gratuitous in the way that the failure to save the stranger's other arm is. This is because, if they had given to a more effective charity, that would have been worse for those who benefited from their donation to the less effective charity.

A CLOSER ANALOGY TO CHARITABLE GIVING?

Another hypothetical example in the philosophical literature that may seem more closely parallel to the Helmsley bequest was presented some years ago by Shelly Kagan (1989, 16):

> Suppose a building is on fire. Upon entering, I find a child and a bird trapped within. Needing one hand free to clear a path back outside, I can save only one of the two, and I hastily pick up— and escape with—the caged bird. Clearly I have done something wrong. Even if [a person with moderate views about doing

good] believes that I was not morally required to risk my safety by entering the building in the first place, he nonetheless believes that once I have decided to undertake the risk, I should have promoted the greater good, by saving the child. If my interests are equally affected by either of two courses of action, I have reason to pick that act with the objectively better outcome.

This case is different from Parfit's in that, if the agent had chosen the option that would produce the greater good, she would not have achieved the lesser good and some additional good as well; rather her saving the child would have excluded the saving of the bird. But the Helmsley case, in which she chose to save many animals rather than many people, may seem just like Kagan's case, only on a larger scale—that is, Kagan's case writ large. If that is right, and if Kagan's judgment about his own case is correct, we should conclude both that Helmsley ought to have donated her fortune to save people rather than to save dogs and that, more generally, people who decide to engage in supererogatory charitable giving then acquire a conditional duty to give to the charity that, according to the evidence they can reasonably be expected to have gathered, would achieve the most good, or prevent or alleviate the most harm.

There is, however, one salient difference between the cases, which is that the agent in Kagan's case seems to save the bird on a mere whim. Just as in Parfit's case there seems to be no reason why the agent might prefer to save only one arm rather than both, so in Kagan's case there is no mention of a reason why the agent might prefer to rescue the bird rather than the child. Helmsley, by contrast, had a reason for saving dogs rather than people, which was that she cared about dogs but apparently rather disliked most people. To make the cases relevantly parallel, we should imagine that Kagan's agent is a bird-loving misanthrope who enters the burning building with the aim of saving the bird. Because this agent cares enough about the bird to risk her life to save it, forgoing saving it would have been an additional cost to her (an opportunity cost) of saving the child.

Kagan concedes that this might make a difference morally. He writes that what his original "case suggests . . . is that although ordinary morality grants me the option to refrain from promoting the good in the pursuit of my interests, I do *not* have the option to react in a manner that neither promotes the good *nor* my interests" (1989, 240). At least according to "ordinary morality," if the agent in Kagan's case has an interest in saving birds but not in saving people (so that it is better *for her* if she saves the bird), it might be permissible for her to save the bird rather than the child. Similarly, Helmsley's interest in saving dogs might have made it permissible for her to devote her fortune to the saving of dogs rather than to the saving of people. And, finally, people who engage in charitable giving often have an interest in the success of a particular charity; for example, it may matter to them to find a cure for a particular disease because someone they loved has died of that disease. In all these cases, then, one might claim that when it is supererogatory to do good at all, it can be permissible to act in a way that does less good if one has an interest in acting that way rather than in another way that would do more good. The explanation for this is that acting in the way that would do more good has an additional cost—namely, the sacrifice of the agent's interest in achieving the lesser good. Because we are assuming that it is the cost to the agent of acting either way that makes her doing any good at all supererogatory, a decision to do *some* good cannot create a duty to produce the greater good if that would require a personal cost that is *even greater* than that which would be necessary to produce the lesser good, which itself is a cost that she is not morally required to accept. (It may be, however, that not every preference or aversion constitutes an interest whose frustration is a relevant cost. I will briefly discuss an example in the section on "The Different Structure of Ordinary Charitable Giving" that raises this issue.)

WHY AN INITIALLY SUPEREROGATORY ACT CAN BECOME MORALLY REQUIRED

Even so, Kagan is right that the agent acts impermissibly in saving the bird. After she enters the burning building, she finds both the child and the bird. At that point she has already taken the relevant risk. She has already made the personal sacrifice that made saving either potential victim supererogatory. Hence she can no longer appeal to considerations of cost as a justification for not saving the child. Saving the child is thus no longer supererogatory. She is now in the position of someone who can save either a child or a bird, though not both, at no cost to herself (or at only a very small cost to herself). Such a person has a duty to save the child, thereby allowing the bird to die. In these conditions, it makes no difference if this person is a misanthropic bird lover who has a personal interest in saving the bird. That interest is sufficiently minor that, if its frustration is the only cost to her of saving the child, this cost cannot justify her failing to save the child.

One might object to Kagan's claim that the agent's action is impermissible by reflecting on the case in the following way. Suppose the agent is among many people who are gathered outside the burning building. Knowing that the risk involved in entering the building is sufficiently great to make it permissible for them not to conduct a rescue, they all decide not to enter—all, that is, except the one agent who dashes in and saves the bird. Can we really believe that, of all these people, the only one who acts wrongly is the only one who has done any good at all—and in conditions in which it was permissible for her not to do any? Although she has done less good than she could have, her failure to do more good is not gratuitous, as there were one or two individuals for whom her doing more good would have been worse—namely, the bird and perhaps herself, if she had an interest in saving the bird but not in saving the child.

This reasoning is specious. As long as the agent remains outside the building with the others, her situation is the same as theirs. But once she is inside the building, her situation is relevantly different: unlike the others, she can save the child at no cost, and it therefore becomes her duty to save it. It is her failure to do so that is wrong. It makes no difference, moreover, how or why she entered the building. She would have had the same duty, once inside the building, even if her being there was the result of the others gathered outside having flung her in against her will.

This explanation of why the agent in Kagan's case must save the child rather than the bird is also the deeper explanation of why the agent in Parfit's case must save both of the stranger's arms rather than only one. It is not in fact essential to his acquiring a duty to save both arms that saving both would involve producing the same lesser good and an additional good as well. Rather, what is essential is that, in saving one arm, the agent has already incurred the cost that made both options supererogatory. He is thus in a situation in which he can save a person's arm at no cost to himself or others. Assuming that he has a duty to save a stranger's arm if he can do so at no cost to anyone, he then has a duty to save the second arm. The situation would be much the same if, having incurred the cost necessary to save stranger A's arm, the agent found that he could either save A's one arm or save both of stranger B's arms, but could not save all three. I believe that he ought then to save both of B's arms, assuming that there is no relevant difference between A and B and that the loss of both arms is at least twice as bad as the loss of one arm. This is so even though, if he were instead to save A's one arm, he would not be *gratuitously* allowing B to lose both arms.

The same explanation applies to a different example presented by Joe Horton:

> Suppose that two children are about to be crushed by a collapsing building. You have three options: do nothing, save one child by allowing your arms to be crushed, or save both children by allowing your arms to be crushed. (2017, 94)

Horton argues with considerable plausibility that *if* one is *willing* to incur the cost of saving one child, it is then one's duty to save both. One's willingness to make the sacrifice necessary to save both makes it obligatory rather than supererogatory to save both. The reason for this, according to Horton, is that our acts must be justifiable to those whom they affect and one could not justify one's failure to save the second child on grounds of personal cost—or, one might add, on any other grounds given the details of the case. I think, however, that the explanation I have offered of why it is wrong to save only one child—namely, that if one saves one child, it then becomes one's duty to save the other because saving the other has become costless—is the more fundamental explanation. According to this explanation, the mere willingness to accept the cost of saving one child does not make it obligatory to save both. The duty to save the second child arises only when and because the saving becomes costless. As we will see later, however, Horton's explanation clearly avoids a problem that mine struggles to avoid.

It does not follow from my explanation in these cases that Helmsley acted wrongly in failing to do what would have prevented the greater harm. When she was choosing whether to leave her money to charities that would care for dogs or to ones that would do more good by preventing the suffering and deaths of persons, she had not yet incurred the cost that made her giving to either type of charity supererogatory (which was mainly just the cost of giving her money away rather than spending it in a way that she might have supposed would posthumously benefit herself, such as having statutes of herself erected at various Helmsley hotels). And the same is true in most cases in which people face a choice between giving to a less effective charity and giving to a more effective one. They do not incur the cost of giving prior to deciding to which charity to give; rather, they incur it when they give, so that their giving to any remains supererogatory. Their choice is thus unlike that which the agents in Parfit's, Kagan's, and Horton's cases face; that is, it is not a choice between doing good at no cost and not doing that good. If potential donors to charity have a duty to give to the most effective charity, it is not for the same reason that the agents in Parfit's, Kagan's, and Horton's cases are required to do more good rather than less.

THE DIFFERENT STRUCTURE OF ORDINARY CHARITABLE GIVING

We can make a simple change to Kagan's case that makes it relevantly parallel to ordinary instances of charitable giving. In Kagan's original case, the child and the bird are in the same part of the burning building. When the agent enters the building, she has immediate access to both and can take either, but not both, on leaving. But suppose the building is large and that the child is near one entrance while the bird is near another. There is insufficient time for the agent to enter the building twice before it collapses. She must choose one of three options: go in one entrance and save the child, go in the other and save the bird, and not go in at all. The reason it is wrong for the agent to save the bird in Kagan's original case does not apply in this version. In both versions, for the agent to be able to save the bird, she must have first incurred the risk of entering the building. In the original case, saving the child is still an option after she has incurred that risk. But in this variant, if she incurs the risk necessary to save the bird, it is no longer possible for her to save the child. In short, in Kagan's case, the sacrifice precedes the choice between acts of saving, whereas in this variant, the choice between acts of saving precedes the sacrifice.

Suppose that in this variant of Kagan's case, the potential rescuer is standing outside the building deliberating about what to do. She knows that it is permissible for her to stay where she is, saving neither. But perhaps because she is a bird lover she dashes into the entrance near the bird and saves the bird just before the building collapses. One cannot claim that she has acted impermissibly because she has failed to save the child when she could have done so at no cost, or only a very small cost, to herself. If she does wrong in saving the bird rather than the child, we still lack an explanation of why that is, given the assumption that it is permissible for her to rescue neither.

Kagan says of his case, "Once I have decided to undertake the risk, I should have promoted the greater good, by saving the child." But merely deciding to take the risk does not seem sufficient to make it obligatory to save the child. It does not become obligatory to save the child until the risk has already been incurred, so that there is no further cost in saving the child. Again, this presupposes that saving either is supererogatory.

Similarly, because the rescuer does enter the building to save the bird in awareness of the risk, we know that just before she does so she is *willing* to accept the risk to achieve the lesser good. Yet it does not seem that, as Horton contends, her willingness to save the bird makes it obligatory for her to save the child instead. We can assume that, because she is a bird fancier, she is motivated to accept the risk to save the bird but not to save the child. Her priorities may be perverse but her passion for birds cannot make it obligatory for her to save the child when saving the child would be supererogatory if she cared less about birds and were unwilling to accept the risk involved in saving the bird. More generally, a contingent motivation, however irrational, to accept a supererogatory cost to produce a lesser good does not make it cease to be supererogatory to accept the same cost to produce a greater good that one is not motivated to produce at that cost.

Horton might be able to accept that it is permissible to save the bird in the variant of Kagan's case, as he concedes that a willingness to make a sacrifice to bring about a less good outcome does not generate a requirement to bring about a better outcome through the same sacrifice *if* one has "adequate agent-relative reasons to favor" the less good outcome (2017, 98). He could, therefore, acknowledge the permissibility of saving the bird in the variant of Kagan's case if a passion for birds constitutes an adequate reason to save a bird rather than a child. Yet I believe, as I am confident that Horton does, that it does not. In Kagan's original case, for example, once the rescuer is inside the building, her being a passionate bird fancier is not an adequate agent-relative reason for saving the bird at no cost rather than saving the child at no cost.

Horton's explanation of the impermissibility of saving only one child in his case is thus limited in scope. It does not , therefore, show that saving the bird is impermissible in the variant of Kagan's case. Yet most charitable giving has the structure of the variant of Kagan's case, not the structure of Horton's case. Hence his explanation of the duty to save both children in his case does not show that there is similarly a conditional duty to give to the most effective charity, unless one has an adequate agent-relative reason to give to the less effective one (2017, 102–104).

OBJECTIONS

There are, as I mentioned earlier, many philosophers who believe, consistently with what Kagan says about his original case, that once one has decided to make a sacrifice by engaging in charitable giving, one ought then to make a reasonable effort to ensure that one does the most good by giving to the most effective charity. These philosophers will be disappointed by my argument to this point, which seems to exonerate Helmsley in her decision to use her wealth to save dogs rather than to save persons. Those who give their time to working at animal shelters rather than raising money to buy malaria nets may, by contrast, feel relieved. But perhaps both reactions are premature, as there are objections to my argument.

One is simply that it is difficult to believe that whether the agent in the burning building cases is morally required to save the child can depend on whether the child is in the same room as the bird or in a different part of the building near a different entrance. That seems morally irrelevant. Yet, odd as it may seem, this is in fact relevant, as it determines whether the agent, having entered the building where the bird is, perhaps with the intention of saving the bird, can save the child at no risk or either can no longer save the child or, perhaps, can still save the child but only at great personal risk. If, as I have repeatedly claimed, she can save the child at no risk, she is morally required to save him, but if the level of risk required to save the child is or remains sufficiently great, saving him is supererogatory.

One possible implication of my argument is that advocates of effective altruism, of whom I am one, might investigate whether the context of charitable giving could be arranged so that it would be relevantly like the situation of the agent who enters the building intending to save the bird but, once there, finds that she has a duty instead to save the child. But it is hard to see how it could be permissible to rig the process of charitable giving so that those who, for whatever reason, want to give to a less effective charity could be led to make their donation only to find themselves morally required to ensure that it goes to a more effective charity instead.

To me it is counterintuitive to suppose that, in the variant of Kagan's case, it could be permissible for the agent to enter the building to save the bird when she could, at no greater risk, go through a different entrance and save the child. But it also seems implausible to me to suppose that, in Parfit's case and the original version of Kagan's case, it is morally impermissible to produce the lesser good, given that it is permissible to produce no good at all. Suppose that in Parfit's case the agent is someone who is willing to save one of the stranger's arms at great personal cost but is, for some reason, simply unwilling to save both arms. It seems perverse to suppose that, given that morality does not require him to save both arms and that, in the absence of such a requirement, he *will not* save both, morality implies that this person may not save one of the stranger's arms when he is willing to do that but must instead choose the permissible option of allowing the stranger to lose both arms.

Here is a rather more intelligible example that illustrates the same problem. Suppose that both a white person and a black person will die unless they are saved. The only person who can save them is a racist. This racist can

A: at some great cost to himself, save the white person;

B: save neither;

C: at the same cost to himself, save both the white person and the black person.

Suppose that, because of the great personal cost of saving either person, option B is permissible. The racist is willing to accept this great cost to save the white person but is simply unwilling to save a black person. Indeed the idea of saving a black person is so repugnant to him that he would rather allow a white person to die than save a black person.

Assuming that morality does not require him to save both and that in the absence of that requirement he *will not* save both, my previous reasoning, which explains and justifies the judgments of Parfit and Kagan about this sort of case, implies that morality forbids the racist to save the white person despite his willingness to do it. I find that impossible to believe. It seems to me inconceivable that morality itself could require the innocent white person to pay with her life for the racist's attitudes.

One might argue that what morality actually requires is that the racist stop being a racist, in which case he would save both. It is certainly true that morality requires him to abandon his racist beliefs and attitudes. But that seems insufficient to solve the problem in this case if anything like the slogan "Ought implies can" is true. For the racist cannot, in this emergency situation, instantly divest himself of the beliefs, attitudes, and habits of a lifetime, thereby becoming at least as willing to save both people as he is to save the white person.

A more promising argument might appeal to the claim that it is only the personal cost of the act of rescue—for example, the inevitability of injury or the risk of injury or death—that makes the act of saving supererogatory. If saving the black person were costless for the racist, morality would require him to do it. Indeed, even though the saving would involve the comparatively minor cost of doing something the racist would find repugnant, morality still requires him to do it. It is only because any of the acts of saving would involve substantial personal cost to the racist that morality does not require him to save anyone, including the black person.

But if it is only this cost that exempts the racist from the duty he would otherwise have to save both, and if his reason not to save both has nothing to do with this cost, perhaps he is not exempted or excused from the duty after all. For he is willing to accept this cost as a condition of saving the white person, and there is no further cost, apart from the repugnance, in saving the black person as well. Considerations of cost are, in effect, motivationally inert. Since the consideration that would release him from the duty to save both is in fact irrelevant to him where saving the black is concerned, he is left with the duty to save both.

Parallel claims apply in Parfit's case and in Kagan's original example. If these claims are correct, they make saving only one arm and saving the bird impermissible but do *not* make it impermissible to save one arm rather than save neither, or impermissible to save the bird rather than save no one, for they also rule out the option of doing no good at all.

The preceding seven paragraphs were written before Horton's article was published and before I had read it. I now recognize, of course, that the last three of these paragraphs are a gesture in the direction of Horton's more sophisticated and far better defended argument, about which I have earlier expressed skepticism. I originally concluded the last of these paragraphs with these two sentences:

> Whether this line of argument is correct is, however, an issue
> I will not pursue further here. It has no application to ordinary

charitable giving, which, unlike these cases, does not offer the option of doing the greater good at no further cost when one has already paid the cost of doing the lesser good.

As I indicated earlier, I still think the second of these sentences is true. I will therefore conclude in the section on "Concluding Thoughts About Philanthropic Giving" with two further gestures in support of effective altruism.

THE ALL OR NOTHING PROBLEM

First, however, I will address the problem raised in the previous section, which Horton calls "The All or Nothing Problem." His article of that title opens with a precise statement of the problem, which is that if, as I think is true in his, Parfit's, and Kagan's cases, it is permissible not to do either act of saving but impermissible to do the act that would do less good, and if one *will not* do the act that would do more good, one is then morally required to do no good rather than the act that would bring about the lesser good. This is because, if one must choose between doing a permissible act and doing an impermissible act, one must do the permissible act. Yet, as I have said, I do not and cannot believe that morality could require one to refrain from saving anyone or anything rather than do an act that would save someone or something of value but would not do the most good one could do at the same cost to oneself and others.

I think there may be a simple solution to this problem, though only in *some* of the relevant cases. First consider Parfit's and Horton's cases. In these cases, it is logically necessary to save one arm, or one child, if one is to save both. Suppose that it is possible to save one arm or child and then to save the second, sequentially, with the entire cost being incurred during the saving of the first. It is clearly permissible, initially, to save one arm or one child. Saving one arm, or one child, becomes impermissible only when one has already acted to save one arm or one child. At that point it is no longer possible to save neither the arm nor the child. And it is at that point that it becomes impermissible not to save the second arm or the second child. Before one has saved one arm or one child, it remains permissible to save neither, and thus permissible not to save the second arm or the second child. That is, when one has not yet acted, it is permissible either to save neither arm nor child or to save one arm or child.

This seems sufficient to avoid the All or Nothing Problem in these cases. It is only when one has saved, or begun to save, one arm or one child, that one is then required to save the second. One has not acted impermissibly in saving one, for after all that is necessary for one to go on to save the other. What is impermissible is, having saved one arm or child, to fail to save the other. When all three options are open, it is permissible to save one arm or one child. But when one's only options are saving one and, at no further cost, saving both, one is morally required to save both. This solution to the All or Nothing Problem emerges from the explanation I have offered of why it is obligatory for one to save the second arm or the second child once one has incurred the cost of saving one.

It also seems to me permissible, though morally mistaken, for the agent to act to save one arm or one child with the intention of saving *only* the one arm or the one child. In acting this way, the agent creates a moral requirement for herself that she intends not to satisfy. But while she can predict that she will wrongly fail to save the second arm or child, she does not, in saving the first arm or child, make it impossible for herself to save the second. Because the act of saving the first leaves open the option of saving the second, it is permissible.

As I indicated, these remarks presuppose the possibility of saving the second arm or child after one has saved the first, thereby incurring the unavoidable cost of saving one or both. But they seem not to apply if, in Parfit's and Horton's cases, it is possible to do only one of three acts: (1) the act of saving neither arm nor child, (2) an act that will save only one arm or one child, and (3) an act that will save both arms or both children. Both Kagan's original case and my variant of it also have this structure, as it is not possible in either of those cases to save the bird first and then save the child.

In Kagan's case, and in Parfit's and Horton's cases when interpreted as allowing only one act of saving, it does seem that there are only two permissible options: saving neither and saving the child, saving both arms or both children. Saving the bird, or saving only one arm or one child is wrong for the reason I have given—namely, that each of these acts involves allowing a child to die, or a person to lose an arm, when one could save the child or the arm at no cost to anyone, or perhaps at the personal cost of saving a child or arm when one is averse to doing so. In the latter case, whether the aversion derives from the opportunity cost of saving a child (as in the case of the bird fancier in Kagan's case) or from a dislike of the potential beneficiary (as in the case of the racist), it is not sufficient to justify one's allowing a person to die or lose an arm.

The All or Nothing Problem in these cases is, again, that if it is supererogatory to save the child or both arms or both children and one is unwilling to do that supererogatory act, the only remaining option that is permissible is not to save anyone or not to save either arm. To respond adequately to this problem in cases of this sort, interpreted as allowing only one act of saving, it may be necessary to draw a distinction between an act's being wrong and its being impermissible. Return to the case of the racist. I agree with Horton that, if the racist is willing to save the white person, he *ought* to save both the white person and the black person. And I believe that he acts *wrongly* if he saves only the white person. But I cannot believe that he *must not* save the white person if, for unjustifiable reasons, he refuses to save the black person. It therefore seems to me that he acts wrongly, but not impermissibly, if he saves only the white person. It may, of course, seem incoherent to suppose that an act can be both wrong and permissible. This suggests that it may be necessary to reject what seems obvious—that the categories of the permissible and the impermissible are mutually exhaustive—and recognize an intermediate category of acts that are neither permissible nor impermissible. Acts in this category ought not to be done because some other act ought to be done instead, but they are not impermissible because it would be morally better to do them than to do some other act that would be permissible. I offer this suggestion without being confident that it is coherent.

CONCLUDING THOUGHTS ABOUT PHILANTHROPIC GIVING

The variant of Kagan's case is morally different from Kagan's own case and from Parfit's and Horton's cases. When the choice among supererogatory acts precedes the sacrifice that makes each act supererogatory, there is no point at which doing the best of one or more initially supererogatory acts becomes morally required because it becomes costless (or insufficiently costly to remain supererogatory). Most instances of ordinary charitable giving are of this sort.

It may be, however, that cases of this sort are amenable to the same understanding that I have suggested for Kagan's, Parfit's, and Horton's cases, interpreted as allowing only a single act of saving. It may be that even in the variant of Kagan's case, it is neither permissible nor impermissible to enter the part of the building where the bird is to save the bird rather than the child. If one is going to enter the building at all, one ought to enter where one will be able to save the child. It is thus wrong to save the bird instead, though it is not impermissible to do so. It is, I concede, less plausible to make this sort of claim about the variant of Kagan's case than it is to make it about the original case. But the form of wrongness that falls short of impermissibility may well admit of degrees.

A different strategy for effective altruists is to try to develop a robust defense of the demandingness of morality, according to which much less of doing good is supererogatory than we have hitherto supposed. It may be, for example, that saving a child, or saving both a white person and a black person, is morally required at a much greater personal cost than we have previously thought.[1]

OTHER PROBLEMS

I have argued that when there are two ways of doing good and both are supererogatory, it is not impermissible to do the one that would do less good. But the reasoning that supports this claim seems to have other implications that are even less appealing. Suppose there are two ways to defend or rescue a threatened person, both equally effective and equally costly, and both sufficiently costly to be supererogatory. If one way would harm the threatener but the other would not, or if one would harm the beneficiary while the other would not, my argument suggests that it would not be impermissible to conduct the defense or rescue in the harmful rather than the harmless way. This is inconsistent with the necessity constraint that governs acts of harming.

Other unwelcome implications emerge in population ethics. Suppose it is supererogatory, or morally optional, for one to have a child. One could either (1) have a child whose life would be well worth living, (2) have the same child in different circumstances in which her life would be worth living but less so, or (3) have no child. My argument seems to imply that it is not impermissible to do 2, even if the cost of doing 1 would be no greater. Finally, suppose the children in options 1 and 2 would be different children. Again my argument seems to imply that it is not impermissible to do 2. This is inconsistent with intuitions typically elicited in cases involving the Non-Identity Problem. Perhaps the implausibility of these implications is mitigated if an act's not being impermissible is compatible with its being wrong because one ought to do a different act instead.

Views that imply that there is a conditional requirement to bring about the best outcome in these cases have a different problem. They have the implausible implication that, if one has decided, permissibly, not to bring about the best outcome, it is then impermissible to do some good rather than none. I hope to discuss these problems in more detail elsewhere.

NOTE

1. The first draft of this paper was presented at a conference on philanthropy and philosophy at the University of Texas at Austin in February of 2015. I am greatly indebted to Sinan Dogramaci for illuminating written comments on that draft. For very helpful written comments on subsequent drafts, I am grateful to Linda Eggert, Ben Sachs, and, especially, Theron Pummer. I am also grateful to Tomi Francis, Adil Ahmed Haque, Thomas Sinclair, and Rhys Southan for stimulating discussion.

REFERENCES

Horton, Joe (2017). "The All or Nothing Problem." *Journal of Philosophy* 114 (2): 94–104.

Kagan, Shelly (1989). *The Limits of Morality*. Oxford: Clarendon Press.

Parfit, Derek (1982). "Future Generations: Further Problems." *Philosophy and Public Affairs* 11 (2): 113–172.

Pummer, Theron (2016). "Whether and Where to Give." *Philosophy and Public Affairs* 44 (1): 77–95.

Toobin, Jeffrey (2008). "Rich Bitch: The Legal Battle over Trust Funds for Pets." *The New Yorker*, September: 38–47.

Chapter 4

Severe Poverty as an Unjust Emergency

ELIZABETH ASHFORD

This chapter discusses the nature of affluent agents' duties toward those whose basic interests are threatened by severe poverty.[1] By "severe poverty," I mean falling below the international poverty line, defined as the line beneath which "a minimally nutritionally adequate diet plus essential non-food requirements are not affordable" (United Nations Development Programme 1996).[2] By "affluent agents" I simply mean agents with enough resources to help without jeopardizing their own or their family members' essential interests. This includes most individuals in affluent countries, and it is the nature of these agents' duties that is my principal focus (though this is by no means intended to exclude other affluent agents from the scope of their duties).

A question that is central to an adequate understanding of affluent agents' duties to those suffering severe poverty is whether they are duties of beneficence or justice or both. The central normative implication of conceiving the duties as duties of justice is that it is not appropriate to frame the duties in terms of how much of our resources we should give. Rather, insofar as we are under duties of justice toward those suffering severe poverty, those resources are not rightfully ours in the first place. Morally they belong to those suffering severe poverty. If the status quo were minimally just, those resources would legally belong to them as well. On this framing of the issue, therefore, it calls for reform of global and domestic economic, political and legal structures, so that those currently suffering severe poverty are no longer deprived of a realistic opportunity to obtain the means of subsistence, to which they are morally entitled.

Discussion of general duties toward those suffering severe poverty has tended to fall into two main categories. On the one hand, there has been a burgeoning literature on the topic of global justice, much of which has focused on ways in which certain features of global economic, political, and social structures significantly contribute to the persistence of severe poverty (the international resource privilege, the arms trade, certain aspects of international trade and finance, debt, environmental degradation, and so on).

On the other hand, much discussion has been triggered by Peter Singer's (1972) arresting and hugely influential argument that our obligations to donate to nongovernmental organizations (henceforth "NGOs") such as Oxfam are at least as stringent as the obligation to rescue a child we happened to pass who is drowning in a pond. As he points out, in both cases we are in a position to prevent a child's death (or some other drastic harm) at relatively insignificant personal cost. His argument has sparked a growing global social movement, known as "effective altruism." It has led to the establishment of charities such as Giving What We Can, GiveWell, The Life You Can Save (founded by Singer), and Good Ventures, which encourage people to donate a substantial proportion of their income to the most effective NGOs and advises them on how they can do the most good with their money.

These two approaches to the nature of affluent agents' duties to those suffering severe poverty have not tended to explicitly engage with one another, but insofar as they have, they have each tended to be skeptical of the other's approach. Those who take affluent agents' duties to the global poor to be duties of justice argue that effective altruism fails to address or challenge the underlying structural causes of severe poverty (see, e.g., Kuper 2002; Kahn 2016). Effective altruism tends to focus on individual affluent agents' capacity to save or transform persons' lives by funding aid agencies to perform specific interventions (such as treatments for neglected tropical diseases), the effectiveness of which can be measured by randomized controlled trials. Critics argue that this moral framing obscures the ways the affluent tend to benefit from structures that harm the poor. They further argue that it is a band-aid approach, which does not address the root causes of severe poverty. Moreover, an objection frequently raised is that NGOs can actually have a detrimental impact on local institutions and politics, and that while randomized controlled trials are good at measuring the effects of specific interventions on targeted populations over a certain time period, they are bad at measuring such long-term macro effects (see, e.g., Wenar 2011; de Waal 1997; Davarajan et al. 2001; Weiss 1998).[3]

Thus Angus Deaton (2015) contrasts the advice he gives to students at Princeton, eager to improve the state of the world, with that offered by Singer. Deaton advises them that rather than donate to NGOs that treat neglected tropical diseases, they should focus their energy and attention on influencing policymakers in Washington to end the policies that are severely harmful to global health (such as the arms trade, agricultural and trade policies, and negotiations that predominantly benefit wealthy and powerful pharmaceutical organizations). Deaton argues that it is absurd for affluent nations to claim to be concerned with global health when we sell arms around the world. As Sir Humphrey dryly remarks in an episode of the British political satire *Yes, Prime Minister*, in response to the prime minister's qualms about a certain arms sale, the bombs could perhaps carry a government health warning.

Effective altruists, in turn, have compellingly argued that we cannot plausibly deny that there are some effective aid agencies, which really could save or transform more lives if we donated to them. Singer (2015) further argues that "sometimes we don't know what the root causes of poverty are" and that "even should we come to know what some of them are, we may still be unable to change them." By contrast, it is clear that an individual affluent agent can save or transform many people's lives by donating to the most effective aid agencies.

The debate, then, has reached something of an impasse. It has been cast in terms of a debate between proponents and opponents of what has come to be known as "the Singer solution" to severe poverty: giving individual donations to the most effective aid agencies. Effective altruism has been characterized by its critics as advocating the Singer solution, and one of the most common criticisms is that it gives inadequate weight to the structural underpinnings of severe poverty.

This may be an inaccurate characterization of the movement. Clearly, if structural reform would do far more good than piecemeal individual donations, and if there were practical steps affluent agents could take to achieve it with a reasonable chance of success, then effective altruism would recommend taking such steps. The two sides in the debate can therefore often seem to be talking past each other.

However, the debate does not simply boil down to an empirical disagreement about how affluent agents can most effectively respond to the suffering imposed by severe poverty. There is also an underlying debate about how affluent agents' duties should be framed. The terminology used by effective altruists, of "giving" and "doing good better," frames the central moral problem raised by severe poverty in terms of an inadequate degree or effectiveness of attempts to do good in the world. The solution focuses on obtaining better evidence about the cost-effectiveness of specific interventions. The implicit assumption is that affluent agents start from a clean moral slate and that the main moral implication of their wealth is the immense amount of good they can do with it.

What underlies many of the objections is the worry that this framing abstracts from and perhaps even obscures the ways in which our wealth has been acquired through global as well as domestic economic and political structures that harm the poor. On this justice-based analysis, the central moral problem raised by severe poverty is not that of an insufficient degree or effectiveness of altruism, but power and interest, in conjunction with a complacent failure to have adequately scrutinized how we benefit from structures and practices that also harm those suffering severe poverty. This shifts the central focus to the injustice of the structures under which affluent agents and other powerful economic actors have control over a huge amount of resources, while those suffering severe poverty are overwhelmingly vulnerable to social and economic forces beyond their control to the point of lacking any realistic means of earning a subsistence income. The solution requires legal and economic reforms that would empower those suffering severe poverty. This kind of reform requires a transformative shift in social mores and moral norms, which requires in turn challenging moral framings under which harmful structures and practices seem both normal and acceptable. As I shall argue, some of the objections to effective altruism can be made sense of only against the historical backdrop of the way development aid came to replace demands for a legally binding claim of justice by countries in the South to some of the riches of empire and to fairer trade deals.

I argue that duties to donate to effective aid agencies should be seen as *backup* duties to aid those who have been unjustly deprived of their economic entitlements. Affluent agents are under both primary duties of justice to reform the structures that underpin severe poverty and backup duties to aid those suffering severe poverty.

It is important to recognize that the persistence of severe poverty constitutes a structural human rights violation that demands complete abolition, and that responsibility for this violation is not plausibly confined to agents and institutions within the poor countries themselves but is shared by agents and institutions in affluent countries. Affluent agents are under an urgent shared duty of justice to bring about the institutional specification and enforcement of global as well as domestic regulations and duties, compliance with which would end severe poverty. Duties to aid those suffering severe poverty would not arise in the first place if the status quo were minimally just; they arise because the primary duties imposed by the human right to subsistence have not been fulfilled. Thus it is built into the characterization of duties to donate to aid agencies as backup duties that the persistence of severe poverty constitutes a mass injustice.

However, their status as backup duties by no means undermines either their urgency or their stringency. For individuals suffering severe poverty, help by an aid agency may be their only remaining hope of avoiding a cheaply preventable drastic harm, such as the death of their child from malnutrition or from an easily treatable disease. In the situation in which we currently find ourselves, prior to the achievement of structural reform, the fact remains that severe poverty poses a threat to the vital interests of a vast number, liable to blight or altogether destroy their lives, and individual affluent agents are able to prevent that threat for many victims, at moderate financial cost.

Another feature of backup duties, I argue, is that their fulfillment is deeply inadequate *in comparison with* implementing primary duties of justice—in this case, not to deprive people of their fundamental socioeconomic human rights in the first place. This highlights that we should not *limit* our conception of the moral demands posed by severe poverty to donating to aid agencies. However, a further feature of backup duties to donate to aid agencies prior to the achievement of structural reform is that they are of the utmost urgency. This framing therefore acknowledges the significance of the considerations that underlie many of the objections to effective altruism (such as that it is a band-aid approach), while showing that they in no way detract from effective altruism's arguments about the importance of donating to effective aid agencies.

I contend, then, that those (such as Deaton) who focus on combating the injustice of the structural underpinnings of severe poverty, and those who campaign for a greater quantity and effectiveness of aid to those suffering severe poverty, should not be critiquing each other. If they do, they are liable to reinforce a natural but inappropriate and damaging paralysis. This occurs when affluent agents think about donating to NGOs, but then consider that doing so would not address the structural causes of severe poverty, and moreover worry that "the aid industry often makes the politics worse" (Deaton 2015). But when we think about the scale and complexity of the structural reforms that are needed, we worry that as individual agents we are unlikely to significantly advance a solution to the problem; in Singer's (2015) words, we consider that "we may . . . be unable to change" the root causes of severe poverty. The paralysis occurs, then, when the appropriate moral response to severe poverty is cast as a choice between seeking structural reform and donating to aid agencies, and each response seems inadequate. As I argue, if affluent agents' duties to donate to aid agencies are understood as backup duties, which agents should fulfill in conjunction with taking steps toward implementing the shared duty of justice to achieve structural reform, the two approaches complement rather than undermine each other, and we can overcome the paralysis.

Section one on "Severe Poverty as a Structural Human Rights Violation" briefly outlines an argument for taking the persistence of severe poverty to constitute a structural injustice, and indeed a human rights violation that demands abolition. Section two on "A Brief Overview of Effective Altruism" offers a brief outline of effective altruism. Section three on "The Duty to Donate to Aid Agencies as a Backup Duty" argues that duties to donate to aid agencies should be understood as backup duties to aid those who have been unjustly deprived of their economic entitlements. Section four on "Objections to Effective Altruism" analyzes and assesses some of the chief criticisms of effective altruism that have been raised. I argue that framing duties to donate to aid agencies as backup duties acknowledges the importance of the considerations that underlie some of the objections that have been raised to effective altruism, while showing that they do not undermine its central arguments about the importance of donating to effective aid agencies.

1. SEVERE POVERTY AS A STRUCTURAL HUMAN RIGHTS VIOLATION

First, it is important to view the existing global distribution of economic entitlements and control over resources in its historical context. Those born into affluent countries are the beneficiaries of enduring economic structures that can in part be traced back to historical processes that enriched the North through the theft of natural and social resources from countries in the South (including through slavery and through a colonial system under which imperial powers were held legally entitled to own the resources of the colonies). The North was also enriched by a process of industrialization that involved using up far more than an equitable share of fossil fuels (still the cheapest form of energy) and of the absorptive capacity of the Earth. Since both of these resources are finite, the North has thereby deprived of their share countries that have not yet fully industrialized.[4] The pursuit of cheap oil and of other domestic economic interests has also led various countries in the North to fund and support the overthrow of many democratic regimes (the United Kingdom in Iran; the USA in Guatemala, Chile, and so on.)

This is not to say that agents in the North should be held guilty for these historical crimes, which they themselves did not perpetrate. It is simply to say that they cannot rightfully inherit economic entitlements without also inheriting the liabilities that the process of their acquisition incurred. Insofar as affluent countries were enriched through the theft of natural and social resources from other countries, they owe some form of financial compensation to those other countries.[5] It follows that some of the resources of affluent countries rightfully belong to other countries. Thus failure to pay the compensation that is owed constitutes (currently legal) theft. Given that many of those countries lack the resources to secure the means of subsistence for all their citizens, this theft contributes to deprivations of the means of subsistence and therefore has devastating consequences.

Turning to present policies, as Leif Wenar (2016) has argued, the principle that "might makes right," which underpinned slavery and colonialism, continues to govern international law regarding the sale of natural resources such as oil. The International Resource Privilege legally entitles whoever has effective control over a country to sell off that country's resources, however brutal and repressive they are, and even if they cannot on any plausible measure be judged to be accountable to the citizens. The resources of a country morally belong to its citizens, and legally belong to them in official international law. However, because such leaders are not accountable to the people, the Resource Privilege does in fact legally entitle those leaders to steal the resources from the people, and it entitles us to purchase stolen goods.

Such leaders have little or no incentive to enable poor citizens to have access to even enough share of the value of the resources to meet their basic needs, precisely because the leaders are not accountable to them. By contrast, these leaders have a strong incentive to spend the money stolen from those citizens on weapons and on buying off the militia in order to consolidate their oppressive rule. Thus an entirely predictable result of the Resource Privilege is that the poor in these countries are deprived of the resources that rightfully belong to them even to the point of being deprived of the means of subsistence. Furthermore another entirely predictable feature is that the poor are actually severely harmed by the resources that have been stolen from them since the money is used on arms for internal oppression or for brutal conflicts over the resources (Wenar 2016; Pogge 2008). At the same time it guarantees affluent countries a cheap supply of oil.

Moreover, while industrialization has predominantly enriched developed countries, the worst effects of the damage it has inflicted on Earth's atmosphere are generally suffered by members of poor and developing countries. In poor countries local crops are the only food source for much of the population. Crop failure through drought or flooding is liable to lead to food insufficiency and threaten vital interests. But even though the North both caused the problem and became enriched by it, it has so far refused to adequately offset the costs of adaptation or of the transition to clean energy.

In addition the North is continuing to draw on an inordinate share of fossil fuels in order to engage in luxury emissions, thereby rapidly depleting an increasingly scarce resource, access to Earth's absorptive capacity. As Shue (2014, 197) points out, as long as the world's energy supply is dependent on fossil fuels, access to Earth's absorptive capacity is a vital resource: "The vast majority of people alive today must, in order to survive, engage in economic activities that generate GHG [greenhouse gas] emissions." In drawing on resources at an unsustainable rate in order to engage in luxury emissions, the North is thereby depriving current and future poor of access to even enough absorptive capacity for subsistence emissions.

The roughly 1 billion people living in high-income counties account for 81 percent of global household expenditure, while the 2.5 billion suffering severe poverty (39 percent of humankind) together account for only 1.6 percent of global household consumption expenditure. The forty-eight least developed countries in the world with a population of nearly 1 billion have a combined GDP that is only a quarter of the GDP of one single developed country, Germany (with a population of 80 million): $870 billion compared to 3.7$ trillion (Arda 2014). Nevertheless rich countries have never paid compensation for the historical processes that enriched them through the theft of natural and social resources from countries now suffering severe poverty. On the contrary, it has been widely argued that rich countries have taken advantage of the superior bargaining power conferred by their wealth and political power to press for rules concerning trade, intellectual property rights, debt, and so on that are skewed in their favor or that of powerful corporations (such as pharmaceutical companies), and unfairly further disadvantage the global poor. Furthermore, as Steiner et al. (1996, 1140) note, certain aspects of the implementation of neoliberal economic policies, "including privatization, deregulation, the expanded provision of incentives to entrepreneurial behavior, and structural adjustment programs and related pressures from international financial institutions and developed countries—have had mixed, and sometimes seriously adverse, effects on the enjoyment of economic and social rights." In addition illicit financial flows from developing countries to tax havens and to richer countries alone exceed development aid (Reuter 2012).

This indicates that certain features of the operation of global social institutions, and of the economic policies of affluent countries and other powerful economic actors, make a significant contribution to violations of the negative duty not to deprive people of the means of subsistence. This is a philosophically straightforward and uncontentious account of the negative duty correlative to the right to subsistence, nonfulfillment of which constitutes a human rights violation.

It should, I contend, be analyzed as a structural human rights violation: the ongoing patterns of behavior of a vast number of agents predictably result in a vast number of victims coming to be deprived of the object of a fundamental human right: the means of subsistence.

As I have argued elsewhere, the positive duties imposed by the right to subsistence, to provide persons with the means of subsistence, should also be seen as general duties of basic justice, owed to every person simply in virtue of their humanity. Given the overall level of global resources, our ongoing shared failure to have eradicated severe poverty is incompatible with minimally adequate recognition of the moral value of the lives that are blighted or altogether destroyed by such poverty. It thus falls below the minimal moral threshold that constitutes, in Shue's (1996, 19) words, "everyone's minimum reasonable demand against the rest of humanity."

I contend, then, that the persistence of severe poverty should be seen as a structural human rights violation and that responsibility for this violation is not plausibly confined to right-holders' own governments but is shared by the international community. An adequate analysis of the structural underpinnings has to have historical depth and has to implicate certain current features of global economic, political, and legal structures. Agents who participate in this structural human rights violation are under an urgent shared duty of basic justice to implement a set of structural reforms that would avoid the harm, underpinned by the abstract general duty of justice not to discard persons' lives. This requires the institutional specification, allocation, and enforcement of a schema of regulations and duties, compliance with which would avoid depriving persons of, or provide them with, the means of subsistence.

A core feature of duties of basic justice correlative to fundamental human rights is that they are rightfully enforced. This is essential to achieving the coordination needed to overcome structural injustice and to solve collective action problems. It is also the appropriate response to persons' moral entitlements. Indeed a test of whether or not legal and economic structures are minimally just is whether they recognize, enforce, and implement duties not to violate fundamental human rights (as was illustrated by the challenge the human right against slavery posed to social institutions that failed to acknowledge and enforce a duty not to enslave people). A further core implication of the rightful enforceability of duties of justice is that their recognition empowers those who would otherwise be utterly vulnerable to threats to their basic interests posed by social and economic forces beyond their control.

Thus one of the most important implications of framing the persistence of severe poverty as a mass injustice is that it presents a fundamental challenge to the moral legitimacy of existing legal, economic, and political structures and calls for a real shift in power between the affluent and those suffering severe poverty.

2. A BRIEF OVERVIEW OF EFFECTIVE ALTRUISM

Singer's (1972) original argument in "Famine, Affluence and Morality" appeals to an analogy with a situation in which an agent passes a child drowning in a pond and is easily able to rescue the child at the mere cost of getting his trousers muddy. As Singer points out, it is clear that the agent is under a highly stringent obligation to rescue the child, which it would be deeply wrong to fail to fulfill. Singer then argues that the reason it would be wrong not to rescue the drowning child also grounds the claim that it is wrong for affluent agents to fail to donate to effective NGOs such as Oxfam; in both cases the agent is in a position to prevent something very bad from happening—a child's death or some other terrible harm—at a relatively trivial personal cost.

Inspired by this argument, effective altruism points out that affluent agents (anyone with an income over £34,000 is in the top richest 1 percent globally) are in a position to save or transform several persons' lives by donating to the most effective NGOs. William MacAskill (2015) has offered a defense of the philosophy underpinning effective altruism in his book *Doing Good Better: Effective Altruism and a Radical New Way to Make a Difference*. The main philosophical difference between Singer's approach and MacAskill's is that MacAskill does not begin from the claim that it would be deeply wrong for affluent agents to fail to donate to effective NGOs.

His approach, rather, is to emphasize the immense amount of good that affluent agents can do if they donate to the most effective aid agencies. He describes effective altruism as "like a 99 per cent off sale. . . . It might be the most amazing deal you'll see in your life." (2015, 28).

3. THE DUTY TO DONATE TO AID AGENCIES AS A BACKUP DUTY

In his influential tripartite analysis of the duties imposed by basic human rights, Shue (1996, chapter 2) argues that in addition to primary duties not to violate the right, such rights also impose two kinds of backup duties. The primary duties, not to violate a basic right, are duties not to deprive right-holders of the object of the right. The second wave of duties are duties to protect people against such deprivations. This centrally involves implementing institutional mechanisms for enforcing the primary duties. The last wave of backup duties are duties to aid those who have already been deprived of the object of the right, as a result of the nonfulfillment of the first two waves of duties.

Affluent agents' duties to donate to aid agencies should, I contend, be seen as belonging to this last wave of backup duties. They are duties to aid those who have already been deprived of a realistic opportunity to earn a subsistence income as a result of unjust global as well as domestic structures. Duties to donate to aid agencies arise because the primary duties not to deprive people of the means of subsistence have been violated, which in turn results in large part from our ongoing shared failure to have fulfilled the duty to implement global norm enforcement mechanisms that would prohibit this. They thus arise because the first two waves of duties have already been violated.

A core feature of this third wave of backup duties is that it would be vastly better for the primary duties to be enforced and fulfilled than for right-holders to come to be dependent on fulfilment of backup duties. Individuals who have already been deprived of any realistic opportunity to earn a subsistence income are unjustly in a desperate situation in which they face deep insecurity about whether or not they will obtain enough subsistence to prevent their own or their children's physical deterioration from malnutrition or from some easily preventable and/or treatable disease. They are likely to be dependent on aid agencies for realizing their most fundamental goals, such as their children's health and survival. Given that aid agencies are likely to be underfunded or unreliably funded and can operate only on a limited scale, it is entirely contingent whether these individuals will be able to realize these goals.

Moreover this position of acute vulnerability and dependency in itself gravely wrongs them. Clearly, then, it would be vastly morally better for persons' right to a realistic opportunity to earn a subsistence income (or be provided with the means of subsistence if they are unable to do so) to be enforced and reliably respected.

Relatedly, as Jennifer Rubenstein (2015a, 85) argues, international nongovernmental organizations (INGOs) are "second-best actors" in comparison with democratically elected governments: "Unlike democratically elected governments, INGOs are not authorized by the vulnerable groups they significantly affect, nor are these groups generally able to effectively hold INGOs accountable (in the sense of sanctioning them)." In addition, "since INGOs are based in wealthy Western countries and their upper-level managers are mostly from those countries . . . their decisions and actions often reflect a limited understanding of the social, political, religious, economic and cultural dynamics of the places where they work" (85).

For these reasons the vital work of INGOs is inadequate *in comparison with* the implementation of global and domestic structural reforms under which each person would be guaranteed the opportunity to obtain the means of subsistence (to a reasonable degree of security). Of particular importance are reforms of the features of global economic structures that weaken the capacity of struggling democracies to fulfill socioeconomic human rights (such as structural adjustment programs against a background of severe scarcity).

However, another core feature of backup duties is that they are of the utmost moral urgency. They are liable to be the only remaining opportunity for persons in a desperate situation to avoid some drastic and cheaply preventable harm, liable to blight or altogether destroy their life. Thus while it is important to critique and seek to reform global economic, political, and legal structures that weaken governments' capacity to fulfil socioeconomic rights, until governments have that capacity it is also essential to support aid agencies. Framing the duties to donate to such aid agencies as backup duties brings out the absurdity of the assumption (which tends to be implicit in certain objections to effective altruism rather than explicitly stated) that acknowledgment of the unjust structural underpinnings of severe poverty implies that we should avoid supporting aid agencies. The logic of this assumption is that since the plight of those suffering severe poverty results from unjust structures that have robbed them of their most basic economic entitlements, so that they are now dependent on aid agencies for avoiding, say, their child's physical deterioration or death from malnutrition, then we should abandon them to their unjust plight. Rather, if backup duties to assist people that have suffered such deprivations are not fulfilled, they will have been doubly wronged; after being deprived of their basic socioeconomic entitlements, they are then abandoned altogether.

It is true that there is also an important practical worry that the work of international aid agencies can have a detrimental impact on local politics and on the development of domestic social institutions doing the same work. There may therefore be a difficult trade-off between supporting international aid agencies doing vital work, and avoiding inadvertently contributing to the undermining of domestic social institutions. However, we should exercise considerable caution before concluding that we should not donate to international aid agencies when they are the only actors on the scene currently in a position to prevent a drastic threat to persons' basic interests.

As I shall now argue, framing duties to donate to aid agencies as backup duties strengthens effective altruists' reply to objections to the movement.

4. OBJECTIONS TO EFFECTIVE ALTRUISM

A Normatively Inappropriate Framing

This is the objection that effective altruism fails to examine or challenge the existing political, legal, and social structures that underpin the persistence of severe poverty. The analogy Singer draws between the duty to donate to NGOs and the duty to rescue a drowning child we encounter abstracts from the structural causes of severe poverty. The analogy has been criticized for thereby shifting attention away from those structural causes (see, e.g., Miller 2007, 233–238, 259–260).

It is further argued that the terminology used by effective altruists reinforces inaccurate assumptions about severe poverty and an inappropriate moral framing of the moral demands it gives rise to by abstracting from and even obscuring ways in which the poor are harmed by certain features of global social institutions

and by the economic policies of affluent countries and other powerful economic actors (Gabriel 2017). A worry with the terms
"doing good" and "altruism" is that they present affluent agents as
saviors of the global poor, saving or transforming their lives through
their generous donations, thereby obscuring the way in which the
affluent benefit from structures that also harm the global poor. Thus
Rubenstein (2015b) argues that effective altruism encourages a
"savior mentality," and Daron Acemoglu (2015) argues that it "sorts
people into the helpers and the helped . . . instead of questioning
what led us here in the first place."

The terms "doing good" and "altruism" also trigger a charity
framing of affluent agents' reasons to aid those suffering severe poverty
as highly commendable but morally optional. It is worth examining,
in this context, the difference between MacAskill's framing of the
issue and that of Singer. Singer's original argument concludes that it is
deeply wrong of us to fail to donate to NGOs—just as wrong as failing
to save a drowning child we encounter. While Singer focuses on positive duties of aid and does not present them as positive duties of justice that ought to be enforced, he completely rejects the charity frame.

MacAskill, by contrast, avoids appealing to the claim that it is
wrong for affluent agents to fail to donate. Instead he appeals to the
fact that their affluence gives them the capacity to save or transform
the lives of several people if they donate to the most cost-effective
NGOs. This may indeed be an important part of the explanation of
the movement's success. Telling people that failing to donate would be
deeply morally wrong (comparable to the wrongness of failing to save a
drowning child they encounter) can trigger defensiveness and resentment. By contrast, appealing to the amazing opportunity that affluent
agents have to do good in the world can be stirring and motivational.

However, there is also a danger in this approach: that it can reinforce the view that the only moral implication of affluent agents'

wealth is the great opportunity it provides to do an immense amount of good. If wealth is seen only in this light, the implicit assumption is that the structures under which affluent agents came to accrue their wealth are acceptable. Indeed if the moral focus is solely on the fact that the more money you have, the more good you are able to do, then the processes by which some come to accrue a vast amount of wealth may even seem benign. This is the worry that underlies Amia Srinivasan's (2015) objection that "MacAskill does not address the deep sources of global misery. Effective altruism doesn't try to understand how power works, except to better align itself with it. In this sense it leaves everything just as it is. This is no doubt comforting to those who enjoy the status quo—and may in part account for the movement's success."

A related worry is with the terminology of giving: *Giving* What We Can, *Give*Well, and so on. If the argument of section on "Severe Poverty as a Structural Human Rights Violation" is correct, this terminology is normatively inappropriate, since the money is not rightfully ours to give. Under a just system of economic entitlements each person would have a realistic opportunity to obtain the means of subsistence. A central feature of duties of justice corresponding to human rights is that they are rightfully enforced. Accordingly one of the most important implications of framing the persistence of severe poverty as a mass injustice is that it challenges the legitimacy of existing legal, economic, and political structures and calls for a real shift in power between the affluent and those suffering severe poverty. Genuine recognition of a human right to subsistence would empower those who are currently vulnerable to economic and social forces beyond their control to the point of lacking any realistic opportunity to earn an income sufficient to provide their family with basic necessities.

It is in virtue of the rightful enforceability of duties of justice that those who criticize framing the moral demands that severe poverty imposes on affluent nations and individuals in terms of development aid or individual duties of beneficence view this framing as overly conservative. As Hattori (2003, 246) puts it, "whereas a liberal project of rights entails a real shift in power from the industrialized states, the moral politics of foreign aid legitimizes the power they already have."

While Singer's original formulation of the argument that affluent agents are under stringent obligations to donate to NGOs certainly avoids the charity frame, he does not take the obligations to be duties of justice that are rightfully enforced. His argument therefore does not challenge the underlying structures of power.

In fact effective altruism can be presented in a way that is compatible with acknowledging the need for structural reform. In appealing to duties of beneficence or philanthropy to give to NGOs, it need not be thereby committed to the view that the money rightfully belongs to us. Rather it can be framed as simply asking the question of what we ought to do with the money that is currently, de facto, in our possession. If affluent agents' duties to donate to NGOs are understood as backup duties, which arise because the primary duties imposed by the human right to subsistence have been violated, it is *built into* this way of framing the duties to donate to NGOs that the status quo is fundamentally unjust. This framing acknowledges that an adequate analysis of the moral implications of severe poverty should acknowledge the urgency of reforming certain features of global socioeconomic structures.

PRACTICAL OBJECTIONS TO EFFECTIVE ALTRUISM

A Band-Aid Approach

This line of objection focuses on the practical implications of effective altruism's framing of the moral demands raised by the persistence of severe poverty. One objection is that it is insufficiently ambitious. What is morally demanded is the eradication of severe poverty, and achieving this requires addressing its root causes. It requires reforming the social, economic, and legal structures that underpin the persistence of severe poverty. It is argued that focusing on funding NGOs to perform specific interventions (such as treatments for neglected tropical diseases) is, at best, a band-aid approach, treating the symptoms of severe poverty rather than tackling its underlying structural causes. As Kirk (2012, 248) puts it, "Charity operates within an understanding of the world as it currently is, and does not reach into realms of radical or systemic change. In other words, 'charity' is too small a frame; it fundamentally restricts the scale of action offered or demanded."

Singer's (2015) reply is that "we should not forget that this will mean saving lives, alleviating hunger or chronic malnutrition, eliminating parasites, providing education, helping women to control their fertility, and preserving sight. Not bad for Band-Aids." This is a compelling response; nevertheless it is unlikely to diffuse the worry that we should not *limit* our moral goal to that of managing and alleviating the terrible effects of global injustice and inordinate economic inequality.

As I have argued, one feature of backup duties is that they are deeply inadequate *in comparison with* the fulfillment of primary duties—in this case, to implement just global as well as domestic social institutions that would avoid depriving persons of the means of subsistence in the first place. It follows that donating to aid agencies is not *on its own* an adequate response to severe poverty but has to be accompanied by recognizing and combating the structural injustice that underpins the persistence of severe poverty.

However, backup duties arise because people have already been deprived of their socioeconomic rights, and in this situation aid agencies save or transform many persons' lives that would otherwise be blighted or altogether destroyed. Singer's framing focuses our attention on the fact that such donations have the same kind of moral importance and stringency as they would in a scenario in which we would find it morally unthinkable to fail to save someone's life.

Thus framing the duties to donate to aid agencies as backup duties recognizes the importance of the moral considerations that underpin the objection that it is a band-aid approach while diffusing the force of the objection.

The Discursive Power of INGOs

This line of objection focuses on what Rubenstein calls "the discursive power" of aid agencies: the power to shape widely held meanings. They exercise this power "when they use terms, images, and concepts . . . in ways that help structure people's perceptions and influence their assumptions about what is normal and natural" (Rubenstein 2015, 71). This highlights the need for caution about the way the choice of terminology (of altruism, giving, and so on) might reinforce inaccurate and complacent assumptions about the causes of severe poverty.

It is further argued that achieving the radical structural reform that would address the root causes of severe poverty would have to be underpinned by a transformative shift in public norms; systemic change requires a supportive public. Insofar as effective altruism abstracts from or even obscures the ways in which affluent agents benefit from structures that harm the poor, there is a danger that it could in fact reinforce an inaccurate and inappropriate moral framing of severe poverty that is in tension with the radical shift in public norms needed to achieve the eradication of severe poverty.

In fact the policy departments within the NGO community are well aware that achieving their public ambition of ending severe poverty, and thereby "make poverty history," requires addressing its structural causes, such as achieving trade reform. They are also, however, well aware that they are "severely constrained by what public opinion permits" (Kirk 2012, 184). As Paul Collier (2007, xii) argues in *The Bottom Billion*, "Without an informed electorate, politicians will continue to use the bottom billion merely for photo opportunities, rather than promoting real transformation." It is therefore crucial that the electorate come to have an accurate understanding of the real causes of severe poverty. This requires challenging inaccurate and damaging attitudes and assumptions about severe poverty.

Framing duties to support aid agencies as backup duties would support the work of organizations such as Oxfam to challenge public perceptions about severe poverty. At the same time this framing highlights the need to engage with the world as it is prior to the achievement of structural reform; backup duties arise because people have already been deprived of their socioeconomic rights and are therefore dependent on aid agencies to avoid some drastic threat to their basic interests.

The Negative Impact on Local Politics and Institutions

A third line of objection is that the recommendations of effective altruism can actually have a detrimental impact on the development of local institutions and public services. As Paul Farmer (2005, 244) argues, as the implementation of certain neoliberal economic policies weakens states' capacity to secure socioeconomic human rights, this poses a trap for efforts to promote global health and human rights:

> As states weaken, it's easy to discern an increasing role for non-governmental institutions. . . . But it's also easy to discern a

trap: the withdrawal of states from the basic business of providing housing, education, and medical services usually means
further erosion of the social and economic rights of the poor.
Our independent involvement must be quite different from
current trends, which have nongovernmental organizations relieving the state of its duty to provide basic services.

Similarly Emily Clough (2015) argues that effective altruism
overlooks the way in which the presence of an NGO and sizable
influx of resources from abroad can induce the exit from the state
sector into a parallel set of institutions or can demobilize political
pressures on the government to build up its own public services.

Effective altruists have responded that while this seems true in
the abstract, it is not true of the recommended charities. In response
to Clough's objection, it can be pointed out that Project Healthy
Children's entire aim is to work within governments that have
expressed a desire to bring about mandatory fortification of staple
foods with micronutrients. Deworm the World's aim is to set up
programs for deworming and then help local governments take over
the running of them. It is also important to emphasize that Oxfam is
very much aware of the fact that certain forms of aid can have a detrimental impact on the development of local institutions and public
services, and it assiduously seeks to avoid this pitfall. For example, it
now buys grain from local farmers so as not to disrupt the local agricultural economy. It also employs local workers in both managerial
and front-line jobs to engage with communities and find out how
their social systems function and what their needs really are.

Of course there may be other INGOs that, while being highly
effective in delivering vital services, also run the risk of pushing
out governments from doing that work. This is one of the many
difficult trade-offs posed by the persistence of severe poverty.

Hutchinson's reply to Clough illustrates the strenuous efforts made by the most effective aid agencies to support rather than undermine local institutions and public health programs. The alternative to supporting such organizations is to accept that before structural reform has been achieved, there is no choice but to abandon victims of severe poverty altogether. As I argued in section on "The Duty to Donate to Aid Agencies as a Backup Duty", we should exercise considerable caution before reaching this drastic conclusion.

The Methodology of Cost-Effectiveness Measurements

A fourth objection is that effective altruism's methodology for measuring the effectiveness of different NGOs is too narrow and liable to focus on the immediate impact of specific interventions on the target group and give inadequate weight to broader, longer-term macro effects on politics and institutions. The method of assessment that effective altruism tends to favor is evidence obtained through randomized controlled trials designed to isolate and measure the effects of specific interventions on the immediate target subjects. Gabriel (2017) argues that this narrow focus has led the movement to concentrate almost exclusively on charities that treat neglected tropical diseases, which is an area in which there is plentiful evidence from randomized controlled trials.

An objection to giving this much weight to randomized controlled trials is that, while they are good at measuring the intended effects on the target group over a certain time period, they are bad at measuring the longer-term unintended effects over the broader population—effects, that is, that fall outside the target group or time frame that the researcher has in mind. Accordingly a frequently raised objection to effective altruism is that in its evaluation of favored organizations it typically examines outcomes only among the individuals targeted by the intervention and fails to adequately acknowledge the unintended institutional and political effects.

Conversely, another worry is that focusing on evidence available from randomized controlled trials can lead effective altruism to ignore or downgrade "other less tangible opportunities to do good" (Gabriel 2017, 463). For example, the impact of political campaigning and of supporting shifts in public norms is much harder to measure. As Gabriel argues, if effective altruism sets itself up as an arbiter of the effectiveness of NGOs, it risks inflicting unwarranted reputational damage to organizations that focus on these less tangible approaches, the impact of which falls outside the scope of the favored methodology for the measurement of effectiveness.

The general line of response to this worry has been that insofar as the recommendations of effective altruism ignores certain effects, it will change its recommendations accordingly. Some parts of the movement have responded to objections to the narrowness of assessments made through randomized controlled trials by expanding the evidence base and incorporating new forms of evidence and analysis. GiveWell has formally distanced itself from the disability-adjusted life year metric and expressed a preference for conclusions "supported by multiple different lines of analysis, as unrelated to one another as possible."[6]

However, there is a further worry that some important effects, including the effectiveness of measures to achieve political change, are extremely difficult and perhaps impossible to measure. Indicators and metrics that reliably measure this kind of impact may simply not exist. The upshot is liable to be that "the more cost-effectiveness is promoted as a standard for large-scale decisions about resource use by INGOs, and the more that funding agencies require proof of cost-effectiveness, the more difficult it will be for INGOs to experiment with activities the cost-effectiveness of which is difficult or impossible to measure" (Rubenstein 2015a, 162).

Another reason effective altruism might end up unduly downgrading the importance of seeking structural reform is the broadly act consequentialist moral framing it tends to favor. Act consequentialism focuses on the impact of the various choices available to *individual agents, taking as given* the background social structures; it asks the question, against that background, Which of that individual agent's choices would have the best consequences? However, structural harms can be seen only by looking at the combined effects of the ongoing patterns of behavior of a vast number of agents; they cannot be seen if we limit our focus to the impact of individual agents' actions, even across a lifetime.

Avoiding structural harms is possible only by acting together; it requires coordination of a level of complexity such that it can be achieved only by the institutional specification and enforcement of a schema of regulations and duties, compliance with which would avoid the harms. Coercive legal enforcement of such a schema is essential to solving coordination and collective action problems, in addition to being the normatively appropriate response to the moral entitlements of those who have been unjustly deprived of them. It would in turn have to be underpinned by a radical shift in social norms, so that harmful practices are recognized as such.

As I argued in section two on "A Brief Overview of Effective Altruism", the duty to end structural harms should be understood as a shared duty of justice. By the term "shared duty," I mean one that is held by individual agents, but each agent has only partial responsibility for its fulfillment. Thus the fundamental duty-bearers are still individual agents; the locus of responsibility is not shifted onto existing social institutions and their official agents. Given that existing social institutions are not adequately discharging their responsibility for preventing structural harms, the responsibility falls back on individual agents to reform them or create new institutions. However, the locus of responsibility lies with individual agents as members of a set of agents who could prevent the harm *if* they achieved this coordinated structural reform rather than with individual agents considered one by one.[7]

The impact of an individual agent's attempts to promote structural reform should be assessed not in isolation but as contributing to a stockpile of impetus for such reform. Sustained commitment by many agents is necessary for reaching the tipping point for a transformative shift in social norms that would underpin structural reform. In this context, then, the criterion of neglectedness in conjunction with tractability might not be the best criteria for determining where agents should direct their attention. Singer argues that even when we know the structural causes of severe poverty "we may still be unable to change them." This is clearly true, if the "we" refers to what individual agents can achieve in isolation. However, a morally salient feature of severe poverty is how cheaply it could be eradicated, relative to the overall level of global institutional and technological resources, if feasible and feasibly achievable structural reforms were implemented.

It Overlooks Considerations of Justice and Rights

In a provocatively titled chapter, "The Moral Case for Sweatshop Goods," MacAskill (2015) considers the question of whether we should boycott clothes made in sweatshops and support bans on sweatshop labor and child labor. He argues that we should not, because poor people are better off in a world where sweatshops exist than one in which they do not. The only reason people choose to work in sweatshops is because the alternatives are worse: jobs that pay even less and involve even longer hours and worse conditions (such as scavenging).

Gabriel argues that "for those who believe that human beings have rights, including a right to adequate protection from dangerous working conditions, things are not so simple. This is because the case for sweatshop labor rests on a morally impermissible trade-off: it improves the economic welfare of many by providing them with a source of income but at the expense of those who are maimed or killed in workplace accidents" (Gabriel 2017, 161). On this objection MacAskill's reasoning ignores the role of rights as protecting individuals against unacceptable interpersonal trade-offs that involve sacrificing their basic interests for the sake of benefits to others.

It could be replied on behalf of MacAskill that the effect of simply banning sweatshop labor and child labor is likely to be worse *for the individual right-holder.* In circumstances of severe poverty, if the only available opportunity to earn the means of subsistence is through sweatshop labor or child labor, then individuals are likely to choose that opportunity because they reasonably judge that their interest in obtaining subsistence outweighs their interest in avoiding terrible working conditions. Responding by implementing a ban therefore overlooks the *intrapersonal* trade-off between the interest in obtaining subsistence and the interest in freedom from terrible working conditions that drives individuals to accept the sweatshop labor or send their children out to work. In these circumstances simply banning child labor or sweatshop labor reduces individuals' range of options and is predictably detrimental to their overall interests. The effect of immediate bans on child labor has been particularly well documented (see, e.g., Basu 1999). As MacAskill notes, it can lead to the children's starvation or to their being driven into even worse forms of work, such as prostitution.

MacAskill's argument does indeed highlight the deep inadequacy of responding to our outrage at the working conditions of sweatshop laborers and the plight of child laborers by simply banning them and boycotting their products without addressing the background severe poverty that drives people to accept such jobs. However, MacAskill infers too quickly that we should acquiesce in sweatshop labor and child labor. An alternative inference is that an adequate response has to include tackling the background severe poverty and implementing structural reforms that make available *better* opportunities to earn a subsistence income and thereby improve the range of available options.

These structural reforms would include labor laws enforcing decent working conditions, and paying adults wages sufficient to provide subsistence for their family without having to send their children out to work as child laborers. A widespread social practice of child labor can drive down adult wages and thereby make it impossible for poor families to support themselves without sending their children out to work. Thus even if, for an individual family, it is beneficial to have the option of sending out a child to work, they might all be better off under structural reforms that included a ban on child labor. This highlights the importance of examining the consequences of general social practices rather than confining the focus to individual agents' choices *taking as given* the background social structures.

This relates to a general criticism of neoclassical economics, the methodology of which underpins many of MacAskill's arguments: that it looks only at the choices that are possible without fundamental structural changes and is thereby too accepting of the status quo. MacAskill takes the background economic structures as given and asks whether poor families are benefited by having the option of sweatshop labor or child labor. Against that background the answer is yes, given that the alternative may be no job at all and complete destitution. However, it is also important to look at the choices that would be possible with structural change.

MacAskill's reply to this would presumably be that the countries in which sweatshop labor and child labor are prevalent currently lack the resources needed to implement these structural reforms. He argues that sweatshop labor plays an important role in countries' economic development that would enable them to lift people out of severe poverty. He points out that sweatshop labor and child labor used to be prevalent in what is now the industrial world and that they played a key role in our economic development.

However, that ignores the fact that the existence of the industrial world in itself constitutes a crucial difference between the situation then and now. As Debra Satz (2010, 169) points out, "a key difference between historical and contemporary cases of child labor is that today the industrial world exists. . . . Different distributions of wealth and power would undercut the need for child labor." In an in-depth study of the economic and normative implications of international labor standards, Christian Barry and Sanjay Reddy (2008, 37) argue that

> international burden sharing can enable developing countries *wholly to avoid the perceived tradeoff between improving labor standards and maximising the gains from trade* [my italics]. . . . For example, a large multinational corporation could identify the labor costs in the factories that supply it, and directly provide countervailing wage subsidies to these suppliers. . . . Alternatively, the government of a developed country that imports goods produced in a developing country that has improved labor standards could in principle pay wage subsidies directly to the firms in the developing country that produce these products for export.

Given the overall level of global resources, the choice poor countries currently face between lifting people out of severe poverty and securing decent working conditions is far from unavoidable; on the contrary, it results from the policies of affluent countries, multinational corporations, global social institutions, and more. These policies should be put under the spotlight. MacAskill's framing of the moral issues raised by child labor and sweatshop labor fails to do so, in only looking at the choices that are possible without changes to those policies. Once we consider the options that could be made available with global structural change, those options are no longer restricted to the choice between sweatshop labor or child labor and destitution.

Sweatshop labor and child labor are severely harmful, relative to uncontroversial moral baselines. We should retain the view that they constitute human rights violations that should not be tolerated. However, we should also recognize that what drives people to accept them is that destitution and physical deterioration from malnutrition are liable to be even worse. For those suffering severe poverty, the status quo of ongoing severe poverty is so bad that they are liable to be made better off than they would otherwise be by treatment that is harmful relative to an uncontroversial moral baseline. In other words, for these individuals the status quo is so bad that the empirical baseline of harm—making someone worse off than he or she would otherwise expect to be in the normal course of events—systematically falls below the moral baseline by which to measure severe harm (making someone much worse off than he or she morally ought to be). Thus while sweatshop labor and child labor are liable to make these individuals better off than they would otherwise expect to be in the normal course of events, in which they suffer physical deterioration through malnutrition or are driven to even worse forms of work (such as prostitution), we should not simply infer from this that sweatshop labor and child labor benefit poor families. Rather we should accept that these practices harm them (relative to an uncontroversial moral baseline) but also acknowledge that complete destitution harms them even more.

This reinforces the argument of section on "A Brief Overview of Effective Altruism," that the persistence of severe poverty should itself be seen as an ongoing structural human rights violation that urgently demands abolition. Prior to the achievement of structural reform, individual agents cannot avoid facing terrible trade-offs, such as the choice between sending their children out to work or risking their physical deterioration from malnutrition. But it is important to focus awareness on the fact that these trade-offs arise because of background structures that constitute a trade-off between the interests of affluent agents and the interests of those suffering severe poverty that is so cheaply avoidable as to amount to the discarding of persons' lives.

EFFECTIVE ALTRUISM "PATERNALIZES" THE GLOBAL POOR

There are several different strands of this objection that are often run together. I now analyze them in turn and argue that we should avoid the sweeping claim conveyed in the oft-used phrase that aid "paternalizes" the global poor.

It Overlooks the Agency of Those Suffering Severe Poverty

One strand of the objection is that "this orientation overlooks poor people's central role in alleviating their own poverty" (Rubenstein 2015b). This is an odd objection. It clearly does not apply to interventions such as Give Directly. It is true that some of the interventions effective altruism funds (unlike Give Directly) are indeed instances of poor people being passive recipients of aid and not playing an active role in improving their situation. But these interventions do not prevent the recipients from actively improving their situation in other ways, and moreover tend to facilitate this; for example, the health improvements facilitated by deworming have significant positive impact on children's education, and adequate nutrition combats the chronic severe lethargy that can be caused by malnutrition.[8]

It Overlooks the Importance of Empowering Those Suffering Severe Poverty

A second strand of the objection focuses not on the role the poor currently play in improving their situation but the role they ought to be empowered to play but currently cannot because the existing structures of power have unjustly deprived them of economic opportunities and entitlements that would give them adequate control over the shape of their lives.

This line of argument is presumably what underpins Catherine Tumber's (2015) objection that

> Peter Singer's case for effective altruism brings to mind Andrew Carnegie, or rather, the well-known criticism . . . that [his] philanthropic largesse was made possible by squeezing value from his workers, deskilling most and forcing them into twelve-hour workdays of low-paid penury. . . . Had Carnegie shared his staggering wealth through decent wages and working conditions rather than built thousands of libraries, working people could have built their own libraries—and much else besides.

The thought here is that the poor ought to be empowered by being accorded the economic resources and opportunities to which they are morally entitled. They would then be in a position to take control over their own lives. The position of acute vulnerability, dependency, and disempowerment they are currently in constitutes in itself a grave injustice.

This line of objection highlights the importance of recognizing that the position of chronic dependency and vulnerability experienced by those suffering severe poverty in itself gravely wrongs them. Aid is no substitute for reforming existing structures of power through the legal enforcement of duties of justice correlative to the right to subsistence, thereby avoiding relations of chronic dependence and vulnerability resulting from unjust distributions of economic opportunities and entitlements. If aid to those suffering severe poverty were to be taken to be an adequate substitute for legal reforms that would empower them to claim and enjoy their economic entitlements, and if giving such aid were held to *exhaust* the moral demands that severe poverty imposes on us, this would be a very important objection.

Once more, however, if aid is understood as a backup duty to help those who have been unjustly deprived of their socioeconomic rights, then the objection does not apply. It is important to distinguish recognition of the importance of empowering those currently suffering severe poverty from the broader claim that aid itself paternalizes the global poor.

It is Linked to an Insidious Moral Hierarchy

It is often argued that the charity frame is closely connected to a moral hierarchy between benevolent givers and grateful beneficiaries. This objection can seem puzzling. It is true that aid can be given in a way that is paternalizing and associated with an insidious moral hierarchy between giver and receiver, but only if the recipients are viewed by the givers as somehow deficient and inferior for being in the situation in which they need the aid.

I suggest the rationale underlying this line of objection can be adequately grasped only if it is viewed against the historical backdrop of the way in which development aid came to replace demands for an enforceable claim of justice by countries in the South to some of the riches of empire in order to be able to realize fundamental socioeconomic human rights in the wake of colonialism and slavery. Development aid subsequently came to be associated with an image of Western experts bringing technical and political expertise to benighted countries out of an enlightened humanitarian moral vision, underpinned by an implicit assumption that the North discovered the secret of prosperity (including technology, innovation, and the rule of law) and now has the role of spreading it across the world. Development aid, in this picture, fails to recognize that the North did not simply discover the secret of wealth but systematically plundered the natural and social resources of other countries, and that the lasting effects of this still blight millions of lives. It also fails to recognize that certain features of current global economic interaction continue to present huge obstacles to struggling democracies (such as through the international resource privilege, debt, environmental damage, unfair trade laws, and illicit financial flows).

So the context in which development aid came to be associated with an invidious moral hierarchy was one in which it came to play the role of a *substitute* for adequate recognition of basic socioeconomic human rights, as imposing legally binding obligations on affluent countries. Specifically there are two connections between development aid, viewed in this context, and an invidious moral hierarchy. First, development aid came to be associated with complacent assumptions about the root causes of severe poverty that focus exclusively on factors internal to poor countries themselves. As I argued in section on "Severe Poverty as a Structural Human Rights Violation," this picture lacks both historical depth and geographical width. As Paul Farmer (2005, 153) argues, "There is an enormous difference between seeing people as the victims of innate shortcomings and seeing them as the victims of structural violence."

Second, whereas duties of justice are owed to the recipient and legally binding, aid is discretionary and widely held to be an expression of virtue; even in Kant's schema of duties, according to which imperfect duties are both stringent and demanding, they are nevertheless classified as "duties of virtue." Accordingly whereas recognition and enforcement of duties of justice empower right-holders to demand what is owed to them, potential beneficiaries of humanitarian duties of aid remain in a position of dependence.

Thus the context in which development aid came to be associated with an invidious moral hierarchy is one in which it came to be viewed as an adequate substitute for recognition of legally binding duties of justice owed by affluent countries, correlative to basic socioeconomic human rights, and the concomitant framing of affluent countries as virtuous for giving development aid (the amount of which is very small relative to their GDP), rather than recognizing the extent to which they are implicated in the persistence of severe global poverty through enduring and wide-ranging economic, political, and legal structures.

However, it is extremely important to avoid conflating these worries about the politics and discursive framings of much development aid with the claim that aid in itself paternalizes the global poor. It is a pervasive fact of human existence that we will be in urgent need of others' help at some points in our lives. For many of us this will be primarily confined to infancy and old age, barring tragic interventions, but for others severe injustice places them in a position of acute and ongoing dependence and vulnerability. It is important to avoid the view that being dependent on others, for either reason, is in itself degrading. It is also important to avoid the sweeping claim that agents who give aid to those in a desperate situation are paternalizing the beneficiaries. Such aid is generally motivated simply by solidarity for our shared human vulnerability and humanitarian concern for the importance of each person's well-being. This is certainly the motivation of effective altruists and of those who work in the aid agencies they support. To accuse those who are, for example, enabling parents to prevent their children's death from malnutrition as "paternalizing" the global poor is indeed a cheap shot.

If duties to donate to NGOs are framed as backup duties, this severs these duties altogether from the context in which aid is linked to an invidious moral hierarchy; the context is one in which development aid *replaces* recognition of legally binding duties of justice, but it is built into the framing of duties to donate to NGOs as backup duties that those suffering severe poverty have been unjustly disempowered. But as long as this structural injustice continues, NGO workers and those who support them are often the only agents directly combating the extreme harms and indignities inflicted by severe poverty.

CONCLUSION

I contend that we should not be choosing between what has been termed "the Singer solution" to severe poverty and the structural reform advocated by those who take the persistence of severe poverty to constitute a grave injustice (or even a structural human rights violation). Rather we need to recognize the moral importance of both approaches.

As I have argued, affluent agents' duties to donate to NGOs should be understood as backup duties, which arise because the primary duties imposed by the human right to subsistence have been ignored. This framing is sensitive to the discursive effects of aid agencies, and would support the campaign work of organizations such as Oxfam to raise public awareness about the real causes of global poverty and to challenge the moral framings under which the structures that lead to severe poverty appear both normal and acceptable. It would also support "the ethics of resistance," which focuses attention on the moral illegitimacy of the background structures that mean that agents on the ground face awful trade-offs, such as between sending one's child out to work or risking their physical deterioration from malnutrition. As I argued in section one on "Severe Poverty as a Structural Human Rights Violation," the features of the background structures themselves that result in severe poverty constitute a trade-off that is utterly gratuitous and so cheaply avoidable, relative to the overall level of global resources, as to amount to the discarding of persons' lives.

As we have seen, many of the worries pressed by critics of effective altruism point to respects in which piecemeal interventions by NGOs fall far short of the structural reforms that would eradicate severe poverty and empower those who are currently unjustly deprived of their most basic economic entitlements. If duties to donate to NGOs are understood as backup duties, the moral force of these considerations is fully acknowledged.

At the same time these considerations in no way detract from the moral urgency of the work of NGOs themselves and of affluent agents' duties to support them. Prior to the achievement of structural reform, it is crucially important to engage with the world as it is. This requires acknowledging backup duties to aid those who have been unjustly deprived of the means of subsistence. Recognition of the injustice of their plight in no way lessens the urgency of the backup duties to respond to it.

I contend that effective altruists and those who take severe poverty to constitute a structural injustice should not be critiquing each other. Each approach is appealing to important moral considerations, and an adequate response has to acknowledge the importance of both approaches.

If we combine the insights and moral framings of both of these approaches to severe poverty, we can overcome the paralysis I mentioned at the beginning of this chapter. The paralysis occurs when, in thinking about our duties to donate to effective NGOs, we zoom out and think about the scale and complexity of severe poverty and the structural reforms needed to eradicate it. Conversely, when we think about achieving these structural reforms, we zoom in and think about how little we can do as individual agents to bring them about.

When we think about donating to NGOs we should zoom in on the fact that by giving moderate individual donations we can save or transform several persons' lives, which is of immense moral significance. An advantage of Singer's pond analogy is that it does focus our attention on this. In this respect it may in fact be an advantage of the analogy that it abstracts from the structural context of severe poverty; if we do zoom out to think about the structural context, there is a danger that we will find its scale and complexity overwhelming and paralyzing. The analogy reminds us that donating to NGOs has just as much urgency as responding to small-scale emergencies, such as rescuing a child we encounter drowning in a pond.

It is also, though, important to recognize the respects in which the persistence of severe poverty differs from standard emergencies, understood as random, rare, and episodic. Far from being random and rare, severe poverty poses an ongoing threat to the basic interests of a particular group of individuals, who from the outset face drastically stunted lives and likely premature death unless they are helped. This threat is both completely predictable and preventable at such small cost, relative to the overall level of global resources, as to be utterly gratuitous. It also has deep historical roots and is coproduced by both global and domestic factors. When we think about achieving structural reform, we need to zoom out; we need to consider the structural underpinnings of severe poverty, and we need to consider the steps we can take as individual agents in the context of a shared duty to implement legal and social reform.

Overcoming the paralysis, then, requires adopting both perspectives. We should recognize that severe poverty constitutes a structural human rights violation and add our voice to the impetus for structural reform, and also recognize the urgency of the backup duties to donate to NGOs. Until structural reform has been achieved, individual affluent agents are also under duties to donate to NGOs that are just as urgent as the duty of easy rescue imposed on bystanders in an emergency situation.

To conclude, severe poverty constitutes an ongoing emergency on a vast scale, but one that predictably results from fundamentally unjust global as well as domestic economic, political, and legal structures. The position of an individual agent in an affluent country can be compared with the position of a wealthy philanthropist in Victorian England, concerned with the conditions of children working sixteen-hour days in factories in extremely hazardous conditions and subject to cruel and often sadistic corporal punishments. Many children did become crippled as a result of the working conditions and were simply sacked and reduced to begging and remaining in a situation of complete dependency.

There are all too many parallels with contemporary child labor. As Satz (2010, 164) points out, "According to the most recent study by the ILO, 171 million working children . . . are routinely exposed to health risks, violent abuse, and probable injuries. Millions of children are beaten, raped, harassed, and abused, suggesting that more than economic motivations are driving employers." Moreover since child labor can have a devastating impact on children's developmental interests, and since child laborers are deprived of an education, this increases the likelihood of their ending up in a position of economic dependency and servility as adults.

The Victorian philanthropist should have used his wealth and influence to support the impetus for structural reform that eventually led to the Factory Acts. In the meantime he should also have acknowledged the importance of donating to organizations that supported destitute children and enabled them to attend school and so on.

Affluent agents should recognize that the persistence of severe poverty constitutes an ongoing structural human rights violation, which imposes on us an urgent shared general duty of basic justice to implement the structural reforms that would achieve its abolition. Until this is achieved, we also have urgent duties to support NGOs in providing for a vast number the only available opportunity to avoid a drastic and cheaply preventable harm that is likely to blight or altogether destroy their lives.

NOTES

1. I thank Hilary Greaves, Michelle Hutchinson, Theron Pummer, and Paul Woodruff for very helpful comments.
2. The international poverty line is specified in purchasing power parity at $1.25 a day. Current multidimensional poverty assessments are available online, at hdr.undp.org.
3. For an argument that aid had has had a positive effect on poverty reduction in countries with a "good policy environment," see, for example, Collier and Dollar 1998.
4. Of course, the latter—the earth's absorptive capacity—will run out much sooner than fossil fuels.

5. In the case of depletion of fossil fuels, the compensation should include offsetting the cost of transition to clean energy; see, for example, Shue 2014.

6. See GiveWell, 'Some more considerations against investment in cost-effectiveness' available at: http://blog.givewell.org/2011/11/04/some-considerations-against-more-investment-in-cost-effectiveness-estimates/ and GiveWell, 'Why we can't take expected value estimates literally (even when they are unbiased)', available at: http://blog.givewell.org/2011/08/18/why-we-cant-take-expected-value-estimates-literally-even-when-theyre-unbiased/.

7. Cripps (2013) describes such duties as "weakly collective" duties; they are duties we have as members of a potential collectivity. Her focus is on duties to avoid the harms inflicted by anthropocentric climate change.

8. I thank Hilary Greaves for this formulation of the response.

REFERENCES

Acemoglu, Daron (2015). "The Logic of Effective Altruism." *Boston Review*, July/August. https://bostonreview.net/forum/logic-effective-altruism/daron-acemoglu-response-effective-altruism.

Barry, Christian and Sanjay G. Reddy (2008). *International Trade and Labor Standards: A Proposal for Linkage.* New York: Columbia University Press.

Basu, Kaushik (1999). "Child Labor: Cause, Consequence and Cure, with Remarks on International Labor Standards." *Journal of Economic Literature* 37 (3): 1083–1119.

Clough, Emily (2015). "Effective Altruism's Political Blind Spot." *Boston Review*, July. http://bostonreview.net/world/emily-clough-effective-altruism-ngos.

Collier, Paul (2007). *The Bottom Billion: Why the Poorest Countries Are Failing and What Can Be Done about It.* Oxford: Oxford University Press.

Collier, Paul and D. Dollar (1998). "Aid Allocation and Poverty Reduction." *World Bank Research Papers.* http://www.worldbank.org/research/aid/background/toc.htm.

Cripps, Elizabeth (2013). *Climate Change and the Moral Agent: Individual Duties in an Interdependent World.* Oxford: Oxford University Press.

Davarajan, S, D. Dollar, and T. Holmgren (2001). *Aid and Reform in Africa.* Washington, DC: World Bank.

Deaton, Angus (2015). "The Logic of Effective Altruism." *Boston Review*, July/August. https://bostonreview.net/forum/logic-effective-altruism/angus-deaton-response-effective-altruism.

De Waal, Alex (1997). *Famine Crimes: Politics and the Disaster Relief Industry in Africa.* Oxford: James Currey.

Farmer, Paul (2005). *Pathologies of Power: Health, Human Rights, and the New War on the Poor*. Berkeley: University of California Press, 2005.

Gabriel, Iason (2017). "Effective Altruism and Its Critics." *Journal of Applied Philosophy* 34 (4): 457–473.

GiveWell, "Some More Considerations Against Investment in Cost-effectiveness." http://blog.givewell.org/2011/11/04/some-considerations-against-more-investment-in-cost-effectiveness-estimates/

GiveWell, "Why We Can't Take Expected Value Estimates Literally (Even When They Are Unbiased)." http://blog.givewell.org/2011/08/18/why-we-cant-take-expected-value-estimates-literally-even-when-theyre-unbiased/.

Hattori, Tomohisa (2003). "The Moral Politics of Foreign Aid." *Review of International Studies* 29 (2): 229–247.

Kahn, Beth (2016) . "Poverty, Injustice and Obligations to Take Political Action." In Helmut Gaisbauer, Gottfried Schweiger, and Clemens Sedmak (eds.), *Ethical Issues in Poverty Alleviation*. Switzerland: Springer.

Kirk, Martin (2012). "Beyond Charity: Helping NGOs Lead a Transformative New Public Discourse on Global Poverty and Social Justice." *Ethics & International Affairs* 26 (2): 245–263.

Kuper, Andrew (2002). "More Than Charity: Cosmopolitan Alternatives to the 'Singer Solution.'" *Ethics and International Affairs* 16 (2): 107–128.

MacAskill, William (2015). *Doing Good Better: Effective Altruism and a Radical New Way to Make a Difference*. London: Faber & Faber.

Miller, David (2007). *National Responsibility and Global Justice*. Oxford: Oxford University Press.

Parfit, Derek (1984). *Reasons and Persons*. Oxford: Oxford University Press.

Pogge, Thomas. 2008. *World Poverty and Human Rights: Cosmopolitan Responsibilities and Reforms*. 2d edition. Cambridge, UK: Polity Press.

Reuter, Peter (ed.) (2012). *Draining Development? Controlling Flows of Illicit Funds from Developing Countries*. Washington, DC: World Bank.

Rubenstein, Jennifer (2015a). *Between Samaritans and States: The Political Ethics of Humanitarian INGOs*. Oxford: Oxford University Press.

Rubenstein, Jennifer (2015b). "The Logic of Effective Altruism." *Boston Review*, July/August. https://bostonreview.net/forum/logic-effective-altruism/jennifer-rubenstein-response-effective-altruism.

Satz, Debra (2010). *Why Some Things Should Not Be for Sale: The Moral Limits of Markets*. Oxford: Oxford University Press.

Shue, Henry (1996). *Basic Rights*. 2d edition. Princeton, NJ: Princeton University Press.

Shue, Henry (2014). *Climate Justice: Vulnerability and Protection*. Oxford: Oxford University Press.

Singer, Peter (1972). "Famine, Affluence and Morality." *Philosophy & Public Affairs* 1 (1): 229–243.

Singer, Peter (2015a). "The Logic of Effective Altruism." *Boston Review*, July/August. https://bostonreview.net/forum/logic-effective-altruism/peter-singer-reply-effective-altruism-responses.

Singer, Peter (2015b). *The Most Good You Can Do: How Effective Altruism Is Changing Ideas about Living Ethically*. London: Yale University Press.

Srinivasan, Amia (2015). "Stop the Robot Apocalypse: Review of *Doing Good Better: Effective Altruism and a Radical New Way to Make a Difference*, by William MacAskill." *London Review of Books* 37 (18): 3–6.

Steiner, H., P. Alston, and R. Goodman (1996). *International Human Rights in Context: Law, Politics, Morals*. Oxford: Oxford University Press.

Tumber, Catherine (2015). "The Logic of Effective Altruism." *Boston Review*, July/August. https://bostonreview.net/forum/logic-effective-altruism/catherine-tumber-response-effective-altruism.

United Nations Development Programme. 1996. *Human Development Report*. New York: Oxford University Press.

Weiss, Thomas G. (1998). "Principles, Politics and Humanitarian Action." *Humanitarianism and War Project*. http://hwproject.tufts.edu/publications/electronic/e_ppaha.html.

Wenar, Leif (2011). "Poverty Is No Pond: Challenges for the Affluent." In Patricia Illingworth, Thomas Pogge, and Leif Wenar (eds.), *Giving Well: The Ethics of Philanthropy*. Oxford: Oxford University Press.

Wenar, Leif (2016). *Blood Oil: Tyrants, Violence, and the Rules That Run the World*. Oxford: Oxford University Press.

Chapter 5

Integrity, Identity, and Choosing a Charity

BRANDON BOESCH

When I was growing up, we always had *so much mail* at my house. Much of this was composed of handwritten letters because my mother (an English teacher) has always fostered a spirited affection for the written word. The rest of the mail was composed primarily of bills and requests for charitable donations: two wildly different sides of contemporary society, united in their pursuit of money. The charitable requests were each rather distinct: here was a religious organization helping the poor in rural central Nebraska (where I grew up); here was a secular organization helping the hungry in some remote part of Central Africa; here was a college requesting funds to build a desperately needed new library; and here was an organization seeking donations to research promising treatments for debilitating illnesses. This was a more or less daily occurrence: extremely different needs being presented to us (or rather to my parents), each with its own meaningful claim to receive donations. How did they ever decide?

I suspect that this situation is not foreign to most people reading this essay. Of course many of the requests for charitable donations have changed medium, from paper mail to digital emails with links to fill out forms to sign up for automatic monthly payments. Nonetheless the bewilderment of charity choice is still a problem for anyone with money to give. Different people react in different ways to wade through the options to decide where they will give their money. I once heard of a family who put all the requests they receive into a box. The requests are then shuffled and one is randomly selected each month. This selected charity wins an arbitrary "charitable lottery," as it were, and is given that month's allocation of funds as the prize. Other methods of choice, which I suspect are much more widely employed, are similarly arbitrary. Some choose to donate on a first-come, first-serve basis, giving to whichever organizations happen to request funds right after the giver receives a paycheck. This is subject to a sort of temporal arbitrariness—why should it matter that these charities happen to request at the right time? Even the generic application of a principle of fairness seems to be somewhat arbitrary. Choosing to donate equally to each and every organization that requests funds, while fair by some measures, ignores all those other charities that have not requested money and, further, treats all of the requests as being equal in importance.

Given the bewilderment when choosing a charity, I am empathetic to these arbitrary means of introducing some structure into our choices about where to give our money. All the same I suspect that when we are acting at our best as charitable givers, we take the time to investigate, research, and make a reasoned decision regarding where we want to contribute our funds. But this raises important questions: What are the reasons that should be part of that decision? What precisely should we be looking for when we are investigating and researching our options? What sorts of factors should play into our decision-making? How do we, as Aristotle (1999, 50 [1120a26]) said so long ago, "give to the right people, the right amounts, at the right time"?

In this chapter I discuss the nature of the reasons that are part of the right kind of practical reasoning about charity choice. I begin with a criticism of a view that takes a comparatively narrow perspective on the sorts of reasons that should factor into this decision-making. This view is a wholesale utilitarian approach to philanthropy, which says that you should *always* give your money to those organizations that can assure the highest utility (and, more important to my argument, would further imply that *the only reason* that is worthy of consideration is concern for the highest utility). I will argue instead that certain causes are potentially more choiceworthy for an agent because of her commitments, her own history and background, and even perhaps certain contingent facts about her (e.g., where she happens to live). I do so by reflecting upon Bernard Williams's account of integrity, noting that we, as moral agents, take on certain moral commitments and identities that are at least in part constituted by the actions done in support of the reasons that undergird these identities. If our only way to nonarbitrarily choose between charities is to resort to pure utility, we lose the opportunity to act for the sake of these reasons. This will alienate ourselves, in a way, from our actions, making ourselves channels for causes and goods with which we do not identify and removing our ability to develop as moral persons. I then provide some examples of the sort of concerns that might reasonably be brought into a charitable giver's practical reasoning. I argue that a concern for integrity extends beyond moral identities and commitments, to include those causes for which an individual has a debt of piety, and even to local causes because of a relationship of citizenship. In doing so I show that there are good, nonarbitrary, nonutilitarian considerations in charity selection. I will close with a brief discussion of the relevance of these insights to some recent trends within philanthropy.

THE UTILITARIAN APPROACH

The view I am advancing in this chapter should be seen partly as a response to a utilitarian account of philanthropy, at least insofar as it seeks to alter (by expansion) the utilitarian's list of potential reasons in decision-making about charitable giving. In order to understand precisely what I wish to deny, it is necessary to examine one utilitarian account in more detail. There are a number of familiar accounts that take up this perspective. Since it is rather well-known, I will take as my example Peter Singer's (2009, 15–16) argument (see also Unger 1996). The basic argument is probably quite familiar, but let me briefly rehearse it:

> First premise: Suffering and death from lack of food, shelter, and medical care are bad.
>
> Second premise: If it is in your power to prevent something bad from happening, without sacrificing anything nearly as important, it is wrong not to do so.
>
> Third premise: By donating to aid agencies, you can prevent suffering and death from lack of food, shelter, and medical care, without sacrificing anything nearly as important.
>
> Conclusion: Therefore, if you do not donate to aid agencies, you are doing something wrong. (Singer 2009, 15–16)

This argument, as it stands, is not yet the wholesale utilitarian argument I am worried about. So far all we have is an argument that charitable donation to agencies that work to reduce pain and suffering is good (or more precisely, that failing to donate to aid agencies is wrong in the absence of something more pressing).

I am not here to deny this point, and indeed it is difficult to imagine anyone who would. What I would like to deny is an added premise. It is not stated as explicitly in the main outline of the argument, but the added premise can be seen implicitly when Singer (2009, 24) discusses charitable giving in the United States, noting that although U.S. citizens do a comparatively good job of donating money, "the largest portion of the money Americans give, fully a third of it, goes to religious institutions, where it pays for the salaries of the clergy and for building and maintaining churches, synagogues, and mosques . . . . The next biggest sector is education, including universities, colleges, and libraries." Singer sees this as a negative fact because it means that monetary donations are not going to end "suffering and death from lack of food, shelter, and medical care" (15) Thus the added premise is something like this:

Added premise: Those causes which do not put an end to suffering and death due to lack of food, shelter, and medical care are not nearly as important as those causes which do.[1]

With this added premise we get the conclusion that we should be donating exclusively to those organizations that do put an end to suffering and death.

Now we have arrived at the wholesale utilitarian account that I wish to deny. This account says that we should be donating our money only to those causes that can best increase the utility of those they are serving.[2] When we go to reason about where to send our money, our considerations should relate only to where our money will have the greatest effect, where effect is understood in terms of ending suffering, pain, and death or otherwise maximizing utility.

On the utilitarian view, the consideration of other, nonutilitarian reasons when making decisions about where to donate our money constitutes an error in practical reasoning. The consideration of organizations and causes that aim at different targets is a failure to recognize and respond to the force of the argument presented above. Whatever action results from reasoning of this sort is likely (though not necessarily) going to be wrong.[3]

Before moving on to criticize this account, let me briefly underscore what I am *not* criticizing. I quite agree with Singer that we (that is, those who have any sort of excess) should be donating much more money to charity than we already do.[4] Of course I also agree that suffering and death from lack of food, shelter, or proper medical care are indeed grave evils that should be righted and that those organizations combating these wrongs are worthy and deserving of our donations. My concern here is centered upon the reasoning and considerations of the ideal charitable giver. Assuming I have read his implicit concerns correctly, the ideal moral agent on Singer's view would not consider anything beyond the utility of each of the potential objects of her charitable donation. In what follows I argue against this view and provide some positive expansion of the reasons and considerations an ideal moral agent might have. I ultimately conclude that there are other causes to which an agent might rightly contribute and, further, that these opportunities to give are central to living and constituting our moral lives.

BERNARD WILLIAMS'S INTEGRITY CRITIQUE

Let me begin my criticism of this wholesale utilitarian account by rehearsing Williams's (1973) argument against utilitarianism from integrity. The critique is seen best through the employment of the well-known example of Jim, who finds himself in a rather undesirable situation. Here are the details:

> Jim finds himself in the central square of a small South American town. Tied up against the wall are a row of twenty Indians, most terrified, a few defiant, in front of them several armed men in uniform. . . . The captain in charge . . . explains that the Indians are a random group of the inhabitants who, after recent acts of protest against the government, are just about to be killed to remind other possible protestors of the advantages of not protesting. However, since Jim is an honoured visitor from another land, the captain is happy to offer him a guest's privilege of killing one of the Indians himself. If Jim accepts, then as a special mark of the occasion, the other Indians will be let off. Of course, if Jim refuses, then there is no special occasion and Pedro here will do what he was about to do when Jim arrived, and kill them all. (98)

The example goes on to make it clear that there is no alternative option that could reasonably work to get Jim out of this circumstance, making it clear, for example, that he cannot get a hold of a gun to save the natives.

What is Jim to do? In this instance, says Williams (1973, 99), utilitarianism tells us that Jim should choose to kill the native; indeed, according to utilitarianism, this is "obviously the right [answer]." Though Williams agrees that the utilitarian answer to this scenario is "probably right" (117), he still finds reason to criticize the approach. As such, the central part of this criticism focuses not on the *action* upon which Jim ultimately decides but rather on the way Jim arrives at that action.[5] The central part of the problem is that the utilitarian reasoning does not consider the fact that "each of us is specially responsible for what *he* does" (99). That is to say, there is a morally salient connection between an agent's reasoning and commitments and the actions he performs.

Williams goes on to explain this in terms of integrity. First he notes that each individual takes up various projects in her life. Some of these are first-order, for example desiring and working for the basic needs (and perhaps also objects of taste) for you and your family and friends (110). Other projects might be deep and serious projects (not just matters of taste) of "an intellectual, cultural or creative character" (110). Finally, there are "projects connected with . . . support of some cause" (111). Those projects with which an agent most deeply identifies can be thought of as commitments she has. If utilitarianism is successful, says Williams, it must say "that if such commitments are worth while, then pursuing the projects that flow from them, and realizing some of those projects, will make the person for whom they are worth while, happy" (113). Thus when considering the maximization of happiness, we are at least partly considering the maximization of these projects.

The trouble is that when considering what to do, an agent's own projects and commitments are part of the consideration, but "only as one lot among others" (115). This entails some likelihood that the decision will require you to abandon your own project for the sake of someone else's project. Of course there are times when this is, in fact, quite reasonable and probably right, where our own projects are of little importance to us or where the alternative projects are so overwhelmingly important. But when we come to those projects that are tied more deeply to an agent and who she takes herself to be, that is, when we come to consider our commitments, this sort of utilitarian reasoning is problematic at best: "How can a man, as a utilitarian agent, come to regard as one satisfaction among others, and a dispensable one, a project or attitude round which he has built his life, just because someone else's projects have so structured the causal scene that that is how the utilitarian sum comes out?" (116).

And here we see the central point of Williams's integrity critique: to ask an agent to take up all and only utilitarian considerations in situations like this

> is to alienate him in a real sense from his actions and the source of his action in his own convictions. It is to make him into a channel between the input of everyone's projects, including his own, and an output of optimific decision; but this is to neglect the extent to which *his* actions and *his* decisions have to be seen as the actions and decisions which flow from the projects and attitudes with which he is most closely identified. It is thus, in the most literal sense, an attack on his integrity. (116)

I agree with Williams that this is no small failure. Ultimately the loss of integrity constitutes a failure to pay attention to at least one thing that matters when deciding what to do: that it is the agent herself who is doing the action. That is to say, it is a morally salient feature of an action that it is performed by *this* agent and not some other. The failure to pay attention to this feature of any action results in, at some level, a failure to account for all of the moral features of the situation. Of course this is not to say that this consideration *alone* will determine what an agent should do in any given situation. There are many things she must consider. However, it does mean that if she ignores this feature of the action, she will be ignoring something of extreme importance and relevance in her moral decision-making.

INTEGRITY AND CHARITABLE GIVING

I hope that the relevance of this critique to the utilitarian account of charitable giving is already relatively clear. The worry in this situation is that, on the utilitarian account of charitable giving, the factors that play a role in the decision of where to donate one's money fail to recognize at least this feature of the situation: that it is *this* agent and not some other that is deciding where to give her money. That is, the utilitarian approach ignores the important connection between the reasoning and commitments of an agent and her action of charitable donation. Effectively the utilitarian account says "Donate all your money to those organizations that are able to bring about the largest increase in utility." But this is to ask an agent to consider as "one lot among many" those causes that constitute strong commitments for the agent. It is to ask her to reason about her decision *sub specie aeternitatis*, but, as Williams (1973, 118) rightly notices, "for most human purposes that is not a good *species* to view it under." She is an agent with commitments, and this is a relevant moral fact that must be considered in her decision-making.

This is seen more clearly in an example. I have a colleague who works to eliminate sex-trafficking. She has in many ways dedicated her life to this cause—so much so that she wants to write a dissertation on some ethical questions surrounding this problem. She and her husband are both graduate students, so I suspect they do not have much money to give, but nonetheless I am quite sure that they give at least some money to this cause. I have not asked about their charitable giving, not only because this would be a weird thing for colleagues to discuss but also because it seems to be a bit of a silly question, given who I know her to be (i.e., given her commitment to this cause). Were I to ask her, "Do you donate money to causes that work to eliminate human trafficking?," I suspect the response would be quite like the response of President Obama when he was asked by the comedian Zach Galifianakis (2014) which country he would be rooting for in the Winter Olympics: "Seriously? I'm the president of the United States. What do you think, Zach?" His response is telling because of the reference to the identity he holds: qua president of the United States, it is utterly obvious that he will be rooting for the country he governs. I suspect that my colleague's answer would be just as direct (though probably more polite) and similarly justified by reference to her identity: qua committed activist against human trafficking, it is obvious that she would do this.[6] Asking her to stop and reconsider—to perform instead a utilitarian calculus—would be to ask her to abandon this commitment, to act as if she were not a committed activist against human trafficking—in short, to act as if she were not who she is.

Before examining a deeper and more fundamental layer that underscores the importance of these considerations, I must first offer some remarks on the notion of identities being employed here. The general point can be seen in an interesting discussion about the notion of allies of individuals who identify as LGBTQ. Especially on college campuses it is common for individuals who do not themselves identify as LGBTQ to identify themselves as allies of those who do so identify. A few years back there was an interesting discussion of the practices associated with the use of this term. Some were concerned that those individuals who identify as an ally would consider their moral work completed with this identification and thus fail to do any meaningful good for the LGBTQ community. This threat is present because being an ally can easily be mistakenly thought of as a sort of label, like a professional certification. But, as it was nicely put by Mia McKenzie, "'Ally' cannot be a label that someone stamps onto you—or, god forbid, that you stamp on to yourself—so you can then go around claiming it as some kind of identity. It's not an identity. It's a practice. It's an active thing that must be done over and over again, in the largest and smallest ways, every day" (quoted in Smith 2013). McKenzie's point is that becoming or being an ally of the LGBTQ community is not accomplished with the application of a label. To become or be an ally, an individual must value and act for the sake of advancing the causes of the LGBTQ community.[7]

Identities work in the same way.[8] We might think of an identity as a sort of label or way of presenting oneself to the world. But as they are being discussed here, identities are not labels. Identities are characterizations of an agent that emerge from an agent's commitments and her actions done for the sake of those commitments. Speaking of an identity is a way of speaking about a set of reasons for which an agent consistently chooses to act. With this reasons-first notion of identity in play, it becomes clear just how these identities are factoring into practical reasoning. Identities are not themselves the objects of choice and action; agents do not (or at any rate should not) act so as to have an identity. An identity, in the relevant sense being discussed here, is a way of characterizing an agent's (likely dispositional or habitual) acting for the sake of some reasons.[9]

It is this second constitutive feature of identities, that of *acting for the sake of one's commitments*, that leads to the deeper importance of this critique to the questions at hand. We are often inclined to think of these identities as holding for contingent reasons, that our values are founded upon experiences without reflection, that our commitments are themselves arbitrary or default. In his now well-circulated commencement address at Kenyon College in 2005, David Foster Wallace noted that our discussion of identities and values often terminates in discussions of tolerance and a commitment to diversity of beliefs. He thinks these are, of course, important points. But according to Wallace (2009, 26–28), if we stop there, we will miss out on deeper questions related to the nature of our commitments:

[We] also never end up talking about just where these individual templates and beliefs come from, meaning where they come from *inside* the two guys. As if a person's most basic orientation toward the world and the meaning of his experience were somehow just hardwired, like height or shoesize, or absorbed from the culture, like language. As if how we construct meaning were not actually a matter of personal, intentional choice, of conscious decision.

Wallace's point, in the context of the commencement speech, was to encourage the graduates to engage in critical thinking about their own "orientation[s] to the world" and recognize that these are within their own control. The point is relevant here because we will misunderstand Williams's point and the concern I am outlining if we think of these identities as being arbitrary, the sort of thing that develops from contingent, nonrational occurrences.[10]

Instead, with Wallace (2009, 28), I wish to suggest that these identities are themselves "a matter of personal, intentional choice, of conscious decision." Wallace is clear: the choice we have over our identities is not to be found in our declaration of a label for ourselves. Exercising choice over the people we are is a matter of both thinking, "learning how to exercise some control over *how* and *what* you think" (53), and acting, "being able truly to care about other people and to sacrifice for them, over and over, in myriad petty little unsexy ways, every day" (120). That is to say, our identities are within our control provided we both actively view the world in an attentive way and that we act according to the commitments these perspectives instantiate. If this is so, then the threat to integrity that Williams identifies in his critique does not terminate in mere alienation from ourselves but includes an inability to develop these identities at all. At a deep level the utilitarian account threatens our ability to exercise any sort of choice over the development of certain sorts of identities, that is, over the possibility of exercising choice in the way we constitute ourselves as particular sorts of persons.

It is important to note that it is not only direct action that allows for the development of identities. It is a nonnegligible feature of these identities that they can be formed also by indirect actions. This is revealed by a telling phrase employed by seemingly every individual seeking monetary support from family and friends to participate in various long-term service projects: "I give by going. You go by giving." This cliché, though perhaps inappropriately used for personal gain on far too many occasions, reveals that there is more than one way to act for the sake of some cause, that both direct and indirect actions are ways of acting for some cause. There is a real sense in which charitable givers can genuinely say that they "go by giving." There is a real sense in which an agent who gives to an organization that feeds the poor can claim that *she* feeds the poor, even though she never puts food in their bowls or indeed perhaps never even sees the individuals who are being fed.

The importance of this point, specifically with regard to charitable giving, is only heightened by the structure of contemporary society.[11] For many individuals in today's world charitable giving is not merely *one among a number* of ways they act for the sake of particular reasons and so are able to develop particular identities. Indeed for many individuals and for many causes, this is the *only* way they can meaningfully act for the sake of these deep commitments. Most people who have excess to give have this excess only in virtue of being engaged in difficult, tiring, and time-consuming salaried jobs. Apart from the forty hours a week they spend at their workplace, many have children to raise, aging parents to care for, plus the general requirements of living a healthy and sane life. Most individuals are simply *unable* to give a significant amount of their time to the causes they care about. This means the way they *are* able to act for the sake of these causes and as a result develop or maintain the related identities is often with the movement of a pen on a check or the typing of a credit card number onto a website. Since charitable giving is often the only way many individuals can act for their deep commitments, to ask individuals to engage in utilitarian calculation would be to rob them of their ability to act for the sake of their commitments and to rob them of their ability to develop identities.

SOME CONSIDERATIONS IN CHARITY SELECTION

I hope I have successfully shown the relevance of the integrity critique to the utilitarian account of charitable giving: the claim that we are to decide where to give our money in light of *only* utilitarian considerations constitutes a threat to our integrity that is to be seen both as a potential sort of alienation from who we take ourselves to be and as the inability to act to develop the identities that emerge from actions done for the sake of these commitments.

The question then arises: What things should an agent pay attention to when she is making a decision about where to donate her money? Let me begin by first emphasizing that I am not advocating that we throw considerations of utility completely out the window. Agents can and should consider where their money will have the greatest effect, where it will be most efficient, which organizations will most effectively use it, and so on. I take it that this constitutes a very central and basic feature of generosity, as can be seen in Aristotle's (1999, 49 [1119b29–1120a4]) discussion of this topic. Thus I am not here to doubt that these sorts of questions should factor into the practical reasoning of the agent.

However, the argument I have been discussing indicates that these reasons alone are incomplete. I will now provide a positive account of some of the other considerations that might factor into these decisions. To do so I will outline just a few considerations that could reasonably be of concern to an agent in many situations. A few short vignettes will point out the role of integrity and the ways in which an agent can and should consider various commitments. The following considerations in no way constitute an exhaustive list but rather are meant to serve as examples of the sorts of reasons I have in mind.

With each vignette I conclude not that the agent must ultimately give to the cause in question but that she must *seriously consider* giving to that cause. By "serious consideration," I mean the sort of consideration that *might* result in giving to that cause. Put negatively, an individual cannot seriously consider giving to an organization if she has already decided that she will give elsewhere. For each of the following vignettes, my conclusion will be that the agent must be able to seriously consider giving to the organization in question, or else the opportunity represents a risk to her integrity. In each case I refrain from identifying precisely what the agent in question should choose because this decision is (as I hope I am showing) extremely complex. My discussion terminates with identifying some of the serious considerations the individual must have in order to avoid threats to integrity.

This notion of serious consideration raises an issue I will briefly point out and then set aside before moving on to the vignettes. The worry is that the sort of consideration I have in mind is applicable only in a very small subset of situations that do not accurately correspond to typical giving practices. All the vignettes discuss an instance of what we might call "de novo giving," in which an individual has set aside some amount of money and *then* considers where to give it, without any prior assumptions, habits, or decisions. But of course this is rarely, if ever, the case. We are creatures of habit, and so we often give to the same organizations we have been giving to for years. In short, our practical reasoning is often the result of decisions made long ago. If this is the case, then the worry is that the following vignettes will fail to reveal meaningful insights for the way people actually give their money.

This point, while worthy of some attention, does not undercut my general thesis, which is that there are good, nonarbitrary, nonutilitarian considerations that bear on charity selection. This is because if it is true that these sorts of considerations are present in those situations in which an agent decides, de novo, where to give her money, then it is a fairly innocuous inference to assert that these same sorts of considerations are valid in those situations where there is habit, prior assumption, or a different structure to the money being given. As such, for the sake of an easier discussion, I ignore this concern in what follows and set up each vignette with the atypical form of de novo charitable giving.

Citizenship

Consider the relationship of citizenship. That is, should an agent give some preference to those who are her neighbors over those who are not? The question of moral distance is not a new one; many have discussed it, going at least back to Francis Hutcheson (1990, 280–283).[12] I will not give an extended discussion here to questions about moral distance. Instead I just want to indicate that citizenship is one of the things that can reasonably factor into practical reasoning about where to give one's money. To see how citizenship might play a role, consider the following situation:

> Clark, a proud resident of Smallville, Kansas, has just won the lottery. His winnings totaled nearly $3 million. Recognizing that this is an enormous sum, far beyond his needs, he decided to immediately donate $2 million. Meanwhile the town of Smallville

is in the midst of a fundraising campaign to build a new community center, which is the current talk of the town. The old one, which is used quite frequently by many different members of the community for weddings, reunions, and community events, is in disrepair. The new community center will allow for the continuation of these community-building activities. Clark is deciding which organizations will receive portions of his donation.

My suggestion is that Clark needs to give serious consideration to his role as a member of the community of Smallville and consider donating some part of the $2 million to the fundraising campaign for the community center. To see why, suppose that he not only decides to give the money elsewhere (which, recall, I think could be the right conclusion) but he does so without ever seriously considering a donation to the community center. It is fairly clear that this would create a rift between Clark and his identity as a proud community member of Smallville. For one, his failure to consider donating to this cause demonstrates a rather different attitude from other residents of Smallville who are heavily invested in the project. Further, the cause is obviously good for the local community, providing a needed venue for interactions among Smallville citizens. An outsider would have good reason to doubt that Clark values the good of Smallville, simply in virtue of this distinction between Clark and the other residents.[13] This is to set aside any public alienation that might come from the Smallville residents, who are unlikely to consider him a committed community member since they know he could have given to the community's cause. So in this example we can see an instance in which a consideration of membership in a particular community might need to be a part of the reasoning about where to donate money. Once again this is not to say that Clark *needs* to donate to the community center (though it might be so). He could maintain his identity and his connection to his local community if he were able to give good reasons why he donated to another cause. But this requires that he countenance his commitment to the community, that he give some explanation for his decision. Arguably this explanation constitutes the sort of serious consideration I have in mind, since the need to give an explanation shows that reasons were needed to explain why it was not ultimately chosen. Ultimately the failure to give serious consideration to this cause alienates his identity as a citizen of Smallville.

Piety

Another consideration that is likely to be of importance in many situations is that of piety. I understand piety as the honor and service due to those individuals or entities to whom we have a debt we could never fully repay.[14] Thus the objects of piety include but are not limited to one's parents, country, and educators. To see why this should be part of the considerations an agent makes, consider the following example:

> Isaac went to a small liberal arts college in the Northeast, which has a fairly small endowment. While in college he studied American literature. The department is relatively small, and each of the faculty members takes a deep interest in both the intellectual development and general well-being of their students (especially of those in the department). Since the college has a small endowment, it asks each department to do some fundraising so as to carry on its departmental work, a fact of which Isaac is aware. Isaac is sitting down at the beginning of the year to decide where he will donate money over the course of the year.

Like the case of Clark, my suggestion is that Isaac should seriously consider his relation of piety to the professors of his department and should therefore think about contributing to his department's funds. A failure to seriously consider this cause would be to act quite like the prodigal son (Luke 15:11–32). A father has two sons, one who stays with his father and one who takes his inheritance (before his father has died) and squanders it in another country. Even for those who are not religious, the parable tells us something important about relationships involving piety. When the prodigal son left with his inheritance he simultaneously affirmed and denied his sonship; he took the benefits of his being the son of his rich father while at the same time moving away from his home and from his role as a son. Already we can see the rift inherent in this sort of action: there is both an affirmation and a denial of the very same role. The same is true, though to a lesser degree, in Isaac's case. He has taken his "inheritance," as it were, and if he does not seriously consider donating to the department he will be denying his "sonship."[15] This is because if he does not (at least) seriously consider donating to the department, he is effectively saying that there is no debt to be repaid. But as the example is written, this is clearly false, since he owes a debt of piety to his professors. His tuition, however high it probably was, is not sufficient to repay the personal concern given to him by his professors. Just as in Clark's case, an external sort of rift might occur as well. The professors might be offended if they learned that Isaac did not even *consider* donating to the department. Thus these relations of piety should factor into decision-making as well.

Moral Identity

Let me point out one final consideration: that of moral identity. I should briefly clarify what I mean, since communal relationships and relationships involving piety are arguably moral identities. I have in mind those commitments an agent might make which she takes to be constitutive of her living a good and moral life, such as environmentalism, feminism, animal rights, education reform, and civil rights. Consider the case of Gianna:

> Gianna works at a local accounting firm, where she makes a modest salary. In college she spent her spare time participating in environmental cleanups and rallying for environmental causes and was an active member in the local chapter of the Sierra Club. The long hours required by her job combined with her responsibilities as a parent prevent her from being able to give much time to this cause anymore, though she still takes it to be an extremely important cause. Though she has little money to donate, she decides at the start of every month where that money will go.

My analysis here will be brief because it follows analogously upon the other examples. Just as before, my claim is that Gianna's environmentalism should play a relevant role in her decision-making. Were she to act without this consideration, it would be to act without integrity, to reason and act as if she did not care about the environment, and in doing so to partially destroy that commitment. This case is different in one important regard: she no longer has the time to act for the sake of the environment as she once did. The potential remaining means of acting for the good of the environment are now greatly reduced, with charitable donation being one of the few remaining avenues open to her. Thus there is not only a threat to her integrity but also a threat to her ability to maintain or further develop her environmentalist identity at all.

ICE BUCKETS AND INTEGRITY

The preceding considerations are meant primarily to apply to questions related to the decision-making of an individual about where to give her money. Before closing I want to provide some discussion of the relevance of my argument to the broader practice of philanthropy, specifically with regard to a recent philanthropic trend. Like most practices, philanthropy is catching up with the modern world through the use of social media. Just as one sign of this, I rarely get physical mail or phone calls from the organizations to which I donate. Instead I receive emails and see tweets and Facebook posts, each of which shares a little success story, gives an outline of a new problem they hope to tackle, or otherwise tries to motivate me to give, or in the case of those organizations that take monthly withdrawals, keep giving (or give more). The benefits to charitable organizations are obvious: presumably the more connected individuals are to some cause (through personal stories and concrete projects), the more likely they are to donate. There are obvious benefits to the benefactors as well: an awareness of the uses of their donations and a closer connection to the causes they support. This is all fine and well.

However, given a recent event there are reasons to worry that the use of social media in a different way might prove to be a bit more insidious. I am thinking here of the "Ice Bucket Challenge," a viral social media charitable marketing campaign in the summer of 2014. It began rather small, with an individual challenging three of his friends to either dump a bucket of ice water on their heads or donate $100 to the ALS Foundation. The idea was that those friends, after completing either option, would challenge three other friends, resulting in a sort of exponential growth of the challenge.

The challenge morphed a little here and there, the most common change in rules being that people chose to both donate money and dump water on their heads in a short video in which they challenged three others. As you might recall, the Ice Bucket Challenge was fairly wide-reaching, and certainly successful with regard to fundraising. (The ALS Foundation [2014] reported that they received an extra $100 million over the thirty-day period in which the challenge was most popular.) I myself rather enjoyed seeing videos of friends and family (most amusingly, my mother) being drenched with cold water.

During the height of the challenge I came to develop a few concerns about this new experiment of philanthropy.[16] One is that viral marketing will become an ever-increasing trend among charities, with each organization strategizing for what new thing or social media strategy will result in higher donations this year.[17] That this is a serious possibility is suggested by an article published in *The Guardian* that asked some marketing experts what lessons we should learn going forward from the Ice Bucket Challenge (Adeyeri et al. 2014). Another piece of evidence can be seen from the fact that the Muscular Dystrophy Association (2015) decided to discontinue its annual telethon; its CEO Steven Derks acknowledged the role of the Ice Bucket Challenge, saying that it "affirmed for us that today's families, donors and sponsors are looking to us for new, creative and organic ways to support our mission." This is not overly worrisome if the resulting donations of these new methods continue to be *in addition* to the other donations that an individual gives over the course of the year. But it is not unreasonable to suspect that if this becomes more common, people may begin to hold off on making donations because they are waiting until the big charitable giving trend happens that year. This would mean their donations would be worryingly arbitrary, like the family who randomly pulls donation requests from a box.

There is a bigger concern, at least as it relates to my thesis, that follows on this point. Namely, when challenged, an individual is asked (with a fair bit of social pressure) to give to a project or cause that was decided by the *challenger*, or more accurately, that was decided by the *original* challenger. But this seems to be an affront to integrity. The causes that the individual takes up in her action to either challenge others by dumping cold water on her head or to make a donation are not flowing from her own commitments. They are not motivated by the reasons that undergird her identity. Instead the reason she gives to the ALS Foundation has little to nothing to do with what she values in the world but is the result (in large part) of some contingent facts about the nature of social media and the decisions of an original individual whom she (most likely) does not know. The concern is not that she decides to give to this organization (as I have said before, this might be the right conclusion); the concern instead is that the reasons and considerations going into this decision have little to nothing to do with her moral commitments or, shockingly, even with the relative merits of the organization.

As the challenge continued to grow, many people altered the Ice Bucket Challenge to fit with what might be thought of as concerns for integrity. For example, I saw some friends who decided to give to the American Cancer Society, given that their lives had been meaningfully impacted in some way or other by cancer. Similarly I saw a number of Roman Catholic friends opt to give to a Catholic medical research foundation (specifying that the funds were to be used for ALS research), so that their funds would not be used on embryonic stem cell research, which would violate their religious commitments. This shows that there are ways to be respectful of concerns for integrity while still welcoming and embracing new trends in charitable giving. All the same, this is at least one example of a way we (both as givers and as organizers of givers) should be mindful of a concern for integrity as we look to the future of philanthropy.[18]

CONCLUSION

As a way of concluding, let me reiterate that it need not be the case that the agent in question actually ends up choosing to act for her other commitments. There are many situations in which the concern for pain and suffering will cause the agent to choose to give to an organization dedicated to ending those problems. In the end, though, the agent must *seriously* consider the possibility of giving to these other options. This involves countenancing her other commitments and being able, at the very least, to offer an explanation of her decision. More often it will likely involve actually giving to the other causes. If she has done any of these things, then there should be little threat to her integrity. If she does not give these questions serious consideration, then the action will be destructive of her commitment.

What does this mean, in the end, for an agent deciding about where she will give her money? Ultimately it means that there is a lot to consider! Giving money to charity requires careful thought, and these thoughts must expand far beyond the mere consideration of where the money will result in the greatest increase in utility. But this should be fairly unsurprising. Our lives are extremely complex. We take up a gamut of heterogeneous commitments and fulfill a wide range of roles. It should be no surprise that our moral lives would be just as complex. And if a full, rich, moral life is complex, then certainly the reasoning and considerations that help us enact that life will be at least as complex.[19]

NOTES

1. This premise is supported elsewhere by Singer, for example in an editorial piece in the *New York Times* he argues against giving money to museums when you could alternatively donate to reduce the spread of trachoma. See Singer 2013.

2. In Singer's argument the greatest increase of utility is presumed to be obtained through the decrease of suffering due to lack of food, shelter, and medical care. Presumably if we could do more good by donating to organizations that had a higher utility, for example those that did important work in reducing greenhouse emissions, then we should give to these organizations instead. See Singer 2013.

3. Of course since the utilitarian is ultimately concerned with the results of the actions, she will not be overly concerned in the sort of reasoning that gets me to the action, if the action does indeed maximize utility. And, as it stands, any given agent might consider a wide range of possibilities but still ultimately decide to give to those organizations that aim at the reduction of suffering and death due to lack of food, shelter, or medical care. The utilitarian concern about this reasoning will be centered on the fragility of the decision—since there was some chance that it would have gone differently this time, there is some chance the reasoning will go differently (and, as a result, wrongly) next time.

4. My argument for this would center more deeply on the notions of community and the virtue of generosity. Nonetheless, the conclusion is quite similar.

5. He makes it clear that he is focusing on the reasoning of the agents in question right after he introduces his examples when he says that the question is not "just a question of the rightness or obviousness of these answers. It is also a question of what sorts of considerations come into finding the answer" (Williams 1973, 99).

6. Parenthetically I can note that while writing this chapter, I asked my colleague for her permission to include this example in my paper and learned that I was, quite unsurprisingly, correct in my suspicions.

7. A related concern goes in a different direction. A heavy emphasis on identities might be discouraging in a lot of ways. Those who are interested in animal rights, for instance, might want to act positively for these causes but may be overwhelmed by the level of commitment being a vegan would require. Here the identity serves to discourage doing smaller actions for the sake of this cause: eating less meat and fewer animal products. Viewing identities in the way I suggest helps to head off these concerns as well.

8. This is unsurprising, since "LGBTQ ally" is certainly one identity that someone might have.

9. This raises an interesting question about the relationship between identities and virtue. I will not address this relationship at length here, except to note that I suspect an identity is a sort of instantiated or particularized virtue. For

example, being an environmentalist or a committed activist against human trafficking seems to be a way of acting from and for the sake of justice.

10. Of course given the notion of identity described above (having commitments and acting for their sake), some identities can be arbitrary, provided they arbitrarily value something and act for its sake. But the point of the reference to Wallace is to show that we can exercise control over these identities: we create and maintain these identities in our choices about how to view the world and how to act.

11. I do not mean to make a claim that it was easier or harder at other points in human history. I mean only to suggest that it is very difficult for many individuals now.

12. For a more recent discussion, *The Monist* 86, no. 3 (2003) was dedicated to the question of moral distance. I will not offer much more commentary on this question since I think it is tangentially related to the issue of citizenship.

13. Notice that if he were just living in Smallville temporarily and did not value his community, there would be little problem in his not considering this cause since he would not be acting against an identity. However, since he has reasons to value his community and its aims, given that he partakes in community events and is proud of his community, neglecting to bring this reason to his deliberations would constitute a considerable failure qua Smallville citizen.

14. I am following St. Thomas Aquinas in his account of piety, though it is admittedly extended beyond what he had in mind. He thinks of piety as responding to a debt that cannot be repaid by justice, namely our existence. In his view, we owe piety in the first place to God, and in the second place to our parents and country. I am extending the notion to include other debts that cannot fully be repaid by justice, in this case, those related to an education. See Aquinas 1485, II-II, Q.101.

15. The example is problematized a bit by the current commodification of education. In some instances of education there is no particular debt of piety since education is treated and enacted much more like a product for which students pay. However, I meant for the example to make it clear that this was an instance of education far beyond a mere exchange of goods for money. If you are still unconvinced, consider instead someone's benefiting from the Boy Scouts or Girl Scouts and donating to that cause.

16. One is related to the vanity-directed nature of the challenge, but the discussion of that topic will be left for another occasion.

17. The ALS Association (2015) has already decided to make the Challenge an annual event.

18. A practical and concrete suggestion: those organizations in the midst of a large fundraising campaign of this sort might explicitly note in a "Frequently Asked Questions" section of their website that individuals with other commitments should feel comfortable giving to other organizations for any

number of reasons. Similarly they might make a point to publicize someone who participates but gives elsewhere, showing their implicit support of this decision. While this is probably a bad business decision, as it would likely reduce their bottom line, it does seem to be a good decision with regard to being a good charitable organization (which is rather unlike a business in quite a number of ways).

19. This chapter was revised thanks to helpful comments from the presenters and attendees of the University of Texas Royal Ethics Conference of 2015.

REFERENCES

Adeyeri, Ed, Simon Skinner, Lauren Ingram, Joe Edwards, and Warren Johnson (2014). "Ice Bucket Challenge: What Are the Lessons for Marketers?" *The Guardian*, August 27. http://www.theguardian.com/media-network/media-network-blog/2014/aug/27/ice-bucket-challenge-lessons-marketing.

ALS Association (2014). "The ALS Association Expresses Sincere Gratitude to Over Three Million Donors." Press release. http://www.alsa.org/news/media/press-releases/ice-bucket-challenge-082914.html.

ALS Association (2015). "The ALS Ice Bucket Challenge Is Back This August." Press release. http://www.alsa.org/news/media/press-releases/als-ice-bucket-challenge-is-back.html.

Aquinas, Thomas (1485). *Summa Theologica*. New Advent. http://www.newadvent.org/summa/3101.htm.

Aristotle [1999]. *Nichomachean Ethics*. Translated by Terrence Irwin. Indianapolis, IN: Hackett.

Galifianakas, Zach (2014). "Between Two Ferns with Zach Galifianakas: President Barack Obama." *YouTube*. https://www.youtube.com/watch?v=UnW3xkHxIEQ.

Hutcheson, Francis (1990). "An Inquiry concerning Moral Good and Evil." In D. D. Raphael (ed.), *British Moralists 1650–1800*. Indianapolis, IN: Hackett, 280–283.

Muscular Dystrophy Association (2015). "MDA Telethon Ends Historic Run, Urgent Fight for Families Continues." Press release. https://www.mda.org/mda-telethon-ends-historic-run-urgent-fight-for-families-continues.

Singer, Peter (2009). *The Life You Can Save*. New York: Random House.

Singer, Peter (2013). "Good Charity, Bad Charity." *New York Times*, August 10. http://www.nytimes.com/2013/08/11/opinion/sunday/good-charity-bad-charity.html.

Smith, Mychal Denzel (2013). "The Case against 'Allies.'" *Feministing*. http://feministing.com/2013/10/01/the-case-against-allies/.

Unger, Peter (1996). *Living High and Letting Die.* New York: Oxford.
Wallace, David Foster (2009). *This Is Water: Some Thoughts, Delivered on a Significant Occasion, about Living a Compassionate Life.* New York: Little, Brown.
Williams, Bernard (1973). "A Critique of Utilitarianism." In *Utilitarianism: For and Against.* New York: Cambridge University Press, 75–150.

Chapter 6

Giving Isn't Demanding

WILLIAM MACASKILL, ANDREAS MOGENSEN,
AND TOBY ORD

In "Famine, Affluence, and Morality," Peter Singer (1972) suggests
two moral principles that concern our obligations of beneficence:

> *Principle of Sacrifice*: if it is in our power to prevent something
> bad from happening, without thereby sacrificing anything of
> comparable moral importance, we ought, morally, to do it. (231)

> *Weak Principle of Sacrifice*: if it is in our power to prevent some-
> thing very bad from happening, without thereby sacrificing any-
> thing else morally significant, we ought, morally, to do it. (235)

Though many people have been persuaded that these are genuine
moral principles, others have been unconvinced. They argue that
these principles are *too demanding*: if we followed them, we would
have to give away most of what we own and spend most of our time
helping others. This, it is alleged, is asking more of us than morality
truly requires.

In this chapter we propose an even weaker principle:

Very Weak Principle of Sacrifice: Most middle-class members of affluent countries ought, morally, to use at least 10 percent of their income to effectively improve the lives of others.

Even though it's even weaker than Singer's *Weak Principle of Sacrifice*, this principle is still revisionary. The nonprofit Giving What We Can (of which two of the authors are cofounders) encourages people to take a 10 percent pledge; this pledge is regarded by most people who hear about it as beyond the call of duty rather than morally required. On average, per capita private donations as a percentage of GDP amount to about 2 percent in the United States (Giving Institute 2017) and 0.5 percent in the United Kingdom (Charities Aid Foundation 2015); even among those donations, only a small percentage is spent on the most effective programs. Even if only half of all people in the United States abided by this principle, an additional USD 612 billion per year would be donated. As a comparison, total global foreign aid spending is only USD 135 billion per year (Organisation for Economic Co-operation and Development 2015).

In this chapter, we argue that the *Very Weak Principle of Sacrifice* is not very demanding at all, and therefore that the "demandingness" objection has not even pro tanto force against it. Whatever one thinks about the demandingness of Singer's two proposed principles, one should therefore endorse the *Very Weak Principle of Sacrifice* and agree that we still have significant obligations to use our income to effectively improve the lives of others.

Our argument in favor of the claim that the *Very Weak Principle of Sacrifice* is not terribly demanding is based on the following two premises:

1. Giving financial resources is not particularly onerous, far less onerous than we intuitively believe.
2. Giving financial resources does a huge amount of good, far more good than we intuitively believe.

We argue for each of these premises in turn, based primarily on empirical evidence from psychology and economics. Before we begin, however, a few clarifications are in order.

First, this chapter is not concerned with the demandingness of *utilitarianism*. Rather it is concerned with the demandingness of a much more specific normative requirement: giving 10 percent of one's income. Too often the issue of the demandingness of our obligations to use some of our financial resources to improve the lives of others has been conflated with the much more narrow view that we ought always to maximize the good. We don't claim that one does *not* have an obligation to give even more; indeed we believe our arguments could plausibly be extended to higher donation levels. But we believe, at a minimum, that the obligation to give 10 percent of our income should be agreed upon by any plausible moral theory.

Second, we restrict our claim to "middle-class members of affluent countries." We define "middle-class" to mean "in the richest 50 percent" by income. We further restrict the scope of our claim to "most" middle-class members of affluent countries in order to account for those who may have unusually high costs of living, such as those with a disability that requires significant ongoing healthcare.

Third, we do not claim that there is anything special about the requirement to donate 10 percent of one's income. Nor do we mean to suggest that the evidence we cite couldn't justify a requirement to donate more than 10 percent. Rather we chose the 10 percent figure because (1) it is very hard to argue that a principle requiring that much would be too demanding and (2) such a principle already has drastically revisionary implications, given how little people do in fact donate.

Fourth, by "effectively improve the lives of others" we have in mind interventions that improve people's lives much more than the typical intervention. As we note below, it costs only USD 2,800 to save a life in a poor country (GiveWell 2015), whereas typical life-saving interventions in a rich country can be a hundred or a thousand times more costly.

The fifth and most important clarification concerns the nature of the demandingness objection. Whether a moral theory or duty is too demanding depends on two things: the costs to the agent of the actions required by that duty and the size of the moral stakes at issue. If the moral stakes are high, morality can be very demanding, without being too demanding. This is represented within commonsense morality. Consider, for example, a slave owner living centuries ago. He would be morally required to free his slaves even if that meant he would lose his family's livelihood. Or consider an innocent person who, through an unfortunate series of events, has been convicted of murder and is on Death Row in Texas. According to commonsense morality, she would be required to lose her life rather than escape, if the only way to escape involved killing an innocent prison guard.

When we assess the demandingness of a particular duty, therefore, we must look at both the costs to the agent *and* the size of the moral stakes. Our argument in this chapter therefore concerns the *ratio* of how much one can benefit others to how much one can benefit oneself.

One might argue that the slave owner and Death Row cases concern potential violations of *justice* rather than violations of *beneficence*, which is all that failing to give 10 percent would involve. However, even those who endorse the demandingness objection agree that there are some duties of beneficence to strangers, and that these can require sacrifices: "There is nothing intuitively objectionable about a morality's requiring a degree of sacrifice for the sake of benefiting strangers" (Hooker 2009, 151). This makes sense. Sometimes duties of beneficence can compete with or outweigh duties of justice, for example in emergency scenarios, where failing to violate some side constraint would result in the loss of thousands of lives. But if justice can generate large moral stakes that result in demanding duties, and duties of beneficence can sometimes compete with or outweigh duties of justice, then beneficence can sometimes generate large moral stakes. This chapter argues that, in comparison with the loss to the donor, the stakes are indeed very large.

Here is one final point of clarification: when the costs of complying with a moral theory's demands are deemed to be too high, it is not always clear what costs are at issue (Kagan 1989). For the purposes of this chapter, we will assume that the demandingness objection is concerned with the sacrifice of individual well-being or individual self-interest, as opposed to moral autonomy (Slote 1985; Shiffrin 1991) or the pursuit of individual projects and commitments (considered apart from their contribution to individual self-interest) (Williams 1973). Unfortunately a full defense of this assumption is beyond the scope of this chapter. But we assume that representing costs in terms of losses in individual well-being represents a highly intuitive understanding of what it means for a moral theory to be overly demanding in asking the agent to bear unreasonable costs. If we can rebut the demandingness worry attached to the *Very Weak Principle of Sacrifice* on this assumption, we will at the very least have gone a long way to rebutting the demandingness worry tout court. With this on board, we can turn to our main argument.

THE COSTS TO YOU ARE SMALLER THAN YOU THINK

In this section we try to estimate the loss in happiness that a requirement to give 10 percent would impose on the agent. We make three claims. First, our intuitions about the costs of giving aren't generally reliable and are biased in systematic ways. Second, the available evidence suggests that the costs of giving are comparatively minor. Third, the evidence also suggests that giving, besides having some costs, also has nonnegligible benefits.

We should note that, in all cases, the data we give concern the relationship between income and happiness *on average*. It may be that, for some people, income is very strongly correlated with happiness; for such people our arguments will be weaker. Similarly for many people the correlation between income and happiness will be weaker than the average; when directed to such people, our arguments will be stronger.

Unreliable Intuitions

Different people have different relationships with money and draw their happiness from different sources. In order to determine exactly how your happiness, or subjective well-being, depends on a certain level of income, some personal judgment is called for. At the same time we need to be aware of our own fallibility. Psychologists have studied our accuracy in predicting the effect of various outcomes on happiness;

these predictions are called *affective forecasts*. They have found that we are not as good at affective forecasting as we might expect.

We *are* generally good at predicting whether an outcome will be pleasant or unpleasant: we know full well that going on holiday is a good time and that going to the dentist is not. The problem lies elsewhere: in our estimates of quantity rather than quality. Our affective forecasts are subject to an *impact bias*: we overestimate the duration and intensity of the pleasant or unpleasant feelings associated with good or bad outcomes (Wilson and Gilbert 2005). For example, people routinely misjudge the negative impact of various medical conditions on people's quality of life (Boyd et al. 1990; Sackett and Torrance 1978). Similarly, lovers overestimate the negative impact of the dissolution of their relationship, academics overestimate the negative impact of being denied tenure, and voters overestimate the negative impact of having their candidate lose the election (Gilbert et al. 1998).

The impact bias also colors people's perceptions of the relationship between income and happiness. Kahneman et al. (2006, 1909) asked a sample of working women in the United States to estimate the proportion of time typically spent in a bad mood by someone with low income (less than USD 20,000); they found the predicted prevalence of bad mood to be "grossly exaggerated." Aknin et al. (2009, 524) found that a representative sample of Americans "vastly underestimated the happiness of people earning lower levels of household income (USD 55,000 and below)." Giving away 10 percent of your income will probably not reduce your happiness by nearly as much as you think.

The Costs of Giving

It is therefore unlikely that giving 10 percent will be as bad as we intuitively predict, given the unreliability of such predictions. But how bad, if at all, is it likely to be?

Cross-sectional studies consistently show that at any given time, within any given country, income is positively correlated with happiness (see Diener and Biswas-Diener 2002: 122–127 for overview and discussion). Thus the World Values Survey has found the percentage of respondents in the United Kingdom reporting above neutral life-satisfaction to be 19 percent higher for high-income groups compared to low-income groups; in France the difference was 29 percent, in the Netherlands it was 6 percent, and the global average was 17 percent (World Value Survey Group 1994).

What, if anything, can we conclude from this regarding the probable effects of giving away 10 percent of income? One might think of this as equivalent to simply exchanging our level of happiness for that attributed by a cross-sectional survey to someone like us within our country whose income is 10 percent lower than our own; more exactly, we might expect to experience a drop in well-being equivalent to the average difference in happiness between someone earning what we earn and someone earning 10 percent less.

There are two problems with this. First, note that cross-sectional surveys demonstrate only correlation, not causation. The existence of a positive correlation between happiness and income might be partly due to the influence of happiness on income: people of a more cheerful disposition might end up wealthier than others. There is evidence to support the existence of an effect of this kind (Diener and Biswas-Diener 2002: 134–135). Similarly the correlation between income and happiness might be partly due to any number of third variables that cause both higher income and higher happiness (Easterlin 2001: 468; see Diener and Biswas-Diener 2002: 128 for general discussion).

Second, we may worry that cross-sectional surveys don't use the best available measure of subjective well-being. In these surveys well-being is typically measured by asking subjects to provide global reports of life satisfaction. For example, they may be asked, "All things considered, how satisfied are you with your life as a whole these days?" However, there exists an alternative technique for measuring happiness, *experiential sampling*, wherein subjects are asked to report their instantaneous feelings of happiness or un-happiness at several points over an extended period of time. It has been argued that experiential sampling provides a superior method of measuring happiness because it overcomes the biases associated with the cognitive capacities required to recollect and aggregate past experience (Kahneman 1999; Stone et al. 1999). The choice of method matters, as the correlation between income and happiness is weakened when global self-report measures are replaced with ex-periential sampling (Kahneman et al. 2006; Diener et al. 2010). If experiential sampling provides a better measure of subjective well-being, then money buys less happiness than studies of life satisfac-tion indicate.

But let's ignore these concerns and consider the degree to which our happiness would drop if we were to infer causation from corre-lation and equate happiness with life satisfaction. The conclusions we draw would then plausibly provide a *lower bound* for the level to which our happiness would drop as a result of donating 10 percent of our income. Now because the correlation between income and happiness is small and nonlinear, it turns out that even very large falls in income result in very modest drops in life satisfaction. Using data from the Gallup World Poll, Stevenson and Wolfers (2013) found that the relationship between happiness and income is log-arithmic: each additional doubling of income is associated with a constant increase in happiness. By looking at their paper we can see that for a citizen of the United States, a 10 percent reduction in income is associated with a loss of about one-tenth of a point in a ten-point scale measuring life satisfaction. We may conclude that

donating 10 percent should produce, *at worst,* a very small reduction in personal happiness.

The Benefits of Giving

Our discussion in the previous section has assumed that donating
10 percent of our income is like earning 10 percent less. But this
assumption is questionable. In relying on this assumption, we would
presume that giving away money to charities that help people in distant countries is as good from the perspective of our well-being as
having never earned that money in the first place or having simply
thrown it away. This seems quite implausible.

To understand how our happiness varies depending on whether
or not we give 10 percent of our income to charity, we need to look
at how happiness varies with different kinds of spending. Notably
the available evidence suggests that spending money on others can
often improve our subjective well-being to a greater extent than
spending money on ourselves (Dunn et al. 2011).

Imagine the following scenario. You are a participant in a psychological experiment; you are given an envelope containing a small sum
of money, which you are asked to spend within twenty-four hours.
The experimenter can assign you to one of two conditions: she
can require that you spend the money on yourself (paying a bill or
buying yourself a treat), or she can require that you spend the money
on others (buying a present for someone or donating the money to
charity). Which condition do you suppose would bring the greatest
happiness: spending the windfall on yourself or on someone else?

If you are like the typical participant in an experiment of this
kind, conducted by Dunn et al. (2008), you will expect that
spending money on yourself brings greater happiness. However,
the experimenters found that subjects in the prosocial spending

condition reported greater happiness after spending their windfall than did those in the personal spending condition. This was not an isolated result. Dunn et al. also conducted a longitudinal study of sixteen employees at a Boston-based company who received a profit-sharing bonus, finding that those who devoted more of their bonus to prosocial spending experienced greater happiness as a result of spending their windfall; a cross-sectional study of a representative sample of Americans also found greater prosocial spending correlated with significantly greater happiness, while personal spending turned out to be unrelated to happiness. Similarly Aknin et al. (2010) examined survey data from 136 countries gathered by the Gallup Organization, to see whether ratings of subjective well-being were positively correlated with donating to charity. Controlling for household income, it was found that in 122 of the 136 countries there is a positive correlation between subjective well-being and answering "Yes" to the question "Have you donated money to charity in the last month?" The authors found that, on average, "donating to charity has a similar relationship to SWB [subjective well-being] as a doubling of household income" (638).

Of course we have to be careful when trying to extrapolate from these results. The Gallup data did not assess the amount given to charity and are correlational. The sums involved in the experiment are insignificant in comparison to donating 10 percent of one's income. The experiment also involved windfall gains: nobody was asked to spend money that they had already planned to spend for their own purposes. And the experimenters did not distinguish between prosocial spenders who spent money on friends and family and those who donated their money to charity. In spite of such limitations, these results lend some credence to the idea that giving money to charity can be a source of life satisfaction that outweighs whatever minor frustrations we might experience from having less money to spend for our own purposes. Anecdotally this is borne out in the experience of the three authors of this chapter.

Although it is difficult to draw any hard and fast conclusions from the foregoing discussion, we seem to have uncovered evidence that complying with the *Very Weak Principle of Sacrifice* will involve no great sacrifice on our behalf and certainly less than we initially expected. If the money we donate is as good from the perspective of our self-interest as money that's straightforwardly forgone, we should at worst expect only a minor decrease in our subjective well-being, on the order of a loss of one-tenth of a point on a ten-point scale. But we've also seen evidence suggesting that charitable giving may bring benefits to us, that these benefits might be greater than we anticipate and greater than those that could be achieved by spending money on ourselves. It is unclear whether donating 10 percent of our income would actually decrease our subjective well-being to any extent. Even if it does, the loss of happiness is far too small to vindicate the claim that requiring people to give this much is particularly demanding.

THE BENEFITS TO OTHERS ARE LARGER THAN YOU THINK

We can assess how much of a comparative benefit we provide to the poor by considering a number of different metrics: (1) the relationship between income and happiness, (2) the cost per life year, and (3) the cost per life saved.

First, let's look at income and happiness. Many of the world's people live in conditions of extreme poverty. They face material conditions that are almost unknown in rich countries, such as the United States and Australia, or in Western Europe. While there is poverty in these rich countries, it is of a very different sort. We are familiar with *relative poverty*, where some people have comparatively less than *others*, which leads to social exclusion, crime, and many other problems. This is a serious concern for these countries, but it is important to distinguish it from what concerns us in this context, which is *absolute poverty*. Absolute poverty is not defined in terms of how much worse off one person is compared to another, but by how little one person has compared to a standard for being able to afford the basic necessities of life.

To put things into perspective, consider that of the seven billion people in the world today:

702.1 million live on less than USD 1.90 per day (World Bank 2015)

663 million lack clean drinking water (World Health Organization and UNICEF 2015)

793 million people are undernourished (Food and Agriculture Organization 2015)

100 million children don't complete primary schooling (UNESCO 2015)

781 million adults cannot read or write (UNESCO 2014)

3 million children will die each year from preventable diseases (UNICEF 2015)

What is important for the present discussion is just that there are a great many people living in extreme poverty, while there are significant opportunities for the more affluent to help alleviate some of their suffering, or to lift some of them out of poverty entirely.

Now consider the world income distribution. Imagine lining up everyone in the world in order of their annual income. There are a couple of technical adjustments that would be required to allow proper comparisons. A dollar goes further in poorer countries, but we can adjust the incomes to take this into account, putting them in *purchasing power parity* terms. There is also a challenge concerning how to account for children, who often have no income. We shall therefore follow one of the typical conventions of dividing up a household's income evenly among its members. Taking these adjustments into account, if you lined everyone up in order of income, you would see the distribution of income depicted in Figure 6.1.

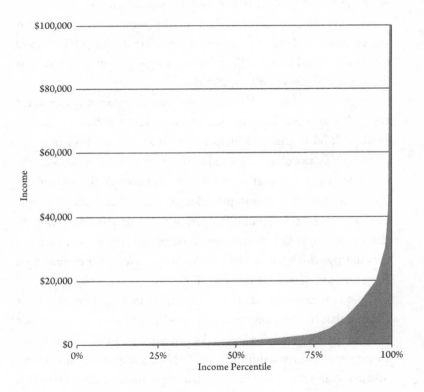

Figure 6.1. Global distribution of income. *Source: MacAskill (2015, 18).*

A perfectly even distribution would appear as a horizontal line on the chart. The actual distribution though, is nothing like this; it is all piled up at the right end of the chart, in the hands of the richest people.

Most people in rich countries do not think of themselves as truly rich. They compare themselves to the people in their social circles and find that they are a little richer or a little poorer. However, on a world scale they are often very rich. For example, a single person in the United States who earned just USD 30,000 per year would be in the richest 2 percent of the world's population and would earn twenty-five times as much as the typical person in the world. Even the current U.S. federal minimum wage of USD 7.25 (USD 14,500 per year) would be enough to leave a single person in the richest 10 percent of the world's population.

Figure 6.1 is one of the most important summaries of the world today. It shows just how unequal the world is; it explains to us our own position in this distribution; and it shows just how little we need each extra dollar compared to the world's poorest people.

Indeed the fact that we've found ourselves at the top of the global income distribution provides us with a tremendous opportunity to make a difference. Because we are comparatively so rich, the amount by which we can benefit others is vastly greater than the amount by which we can benefit ourselves. We can therefore do a huge amount of good at relatively little cost.

Just how much good should we expect to be able to do? Let's assume that by donating to an effective charity we make ourselves a dollar poorer and thereby make a poor person in Africa living in extreme poverty a dollar richer. (This assumption is at least realistic for donations to charities that make direct cash transfers; if you donate USD 1 to GiveDirectly, someone in Kenya or Uganda will receive about USD 0.90.) How much greater a benefit would that dollar provide for the poor African than it would provide for ourselves?

To answer this we can return to economics research on income and well-being. In order to work out the relationship between level of income and level of subjective well-being, economists have conducted large-scale surveys of income levels and the subjective well-being of people in each of them. Their results are given in Figure 6.2, which shows the relationship between income and subjective well-being both within a country and across countries.

The vertical axis of Figure 6.2 represents self-reported life satisfaction. Those interviewed had to say how satisfied they were with their lives on a scale from 0 to 10. Rating yourself at 10 means you consider yourself maximally happy: you think that, realistically,

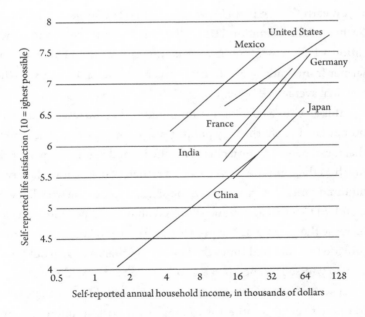

Figure 6.2. Life satisfaction and income. *Source: Stevenson and Wolfers (2013).*

life couldn't get any better. Rating yourself at 0 means you consider yourself maximally unhappy: you think that, realistically, life couldn't get any worse. Most people fall in the middle of this range. The horizontal axis represents annual income.

What's interesting about this graph is that a doubling of income will always increase reported subjective well-being by the same amount. For someone earning USD 1,000 per year, a USD 1,000 pay rise generates the same increase in happiness as does a USD 2,000 pay rise for someone earning USD 2,000 per year, or a USD 80,000 pay rise for someone already earning USD 80,000 per year. And so on.

The economic studies suggest that the benefit you get from having your salary doubled is the same as the benefit an extremely poor person from Somalia gets from having his or her salary doubled. If you earn the median U.S. wage of USD 28,850 per year (Social Security Administration 2014), the benefit you'd get from an additional USD 28,850 in income is the same as the benefit a poor farmer from Somalia would get from an additional USD 133—the nominal average GDP per capita (UNdata 2015).

This gives us a good reason for thinking that the same amount of money can benefit the very poorest people in the world *much* more that it can benefit typical citizens of the United States. If you earn as much as the typical American worker, then you are more than two hundred times as rich as the very poorest people in the world. If you earn USD 28,850 and reduce your income by 10 percent, you can increase the income of 216 people by 10 percent. You will therefore provide two hundred times the benefit to others as you would provide to yourself by spending that money self-interestedly.

A second way of estimating the relative benefit one can provide to oneself versus to others is to look at the cost in different countries of providing one quality-adjusted life-year (QALY), which represents the benefit of giving one person one year of very healthy life. Health economists have estimated the cost of providing one QALY by funding different sorts of health programs or treatments, in order to advise governments on how they can most effectively use their limited resources.

In the United Kingdom the marginal cost to provide one QALY is USD 42,000 (National Institute for Health and Care Excellence 2014, sect. 7.7.). No U.S. agency gives an explicit figure, but Braithwaite et al. (2008) have estimated the societal willingness to pay for health care in the United States at between USD 183,000 and USD 264,000 per life-year. In turn Tengs et al. (1995) analyzed five hundred life-saving interventions in the United States and found that the median intervention costs USD 42,000 per life-year saved.

By donating to the most effective charities, in contrast, one can provide one QALY for as little as USD 100 in poorer countries (GiveWell 2015). Thus for the price we in rich countries are prepared to pay for a single year of healthy life, we could instead provide hundreds of years of healthy life to people in the poorest countries. As with the relationship between income and happiness, the benefit our money could provide for us compared to how much it could provide those in poverty differs by more than two orders of magnitude.

A third way of comparing the benefit one can provide for oneself versus others is to look at the cost to save a life in different countries. Government departments in the United States will pay for infrastructure to improve safety if doing so costs less than about USD 7 million per life saved; the precise figures are USD 9.1 million for the Environmental Protection Agency, USD 7.9 million for the Food and Drug Administration, and USD 6 million for the Department of Transportation.

In contrast, in poor countries, it costs only USD 2,800 to prevent the loss of a life (GiveWell 2015). Here the discrepancy in benefit is even greater: the cost of preventing the loss of a life overseas is less than a thousand times the cost the United States is willing to incur to save the life of an American.

Given these facts, it is hard to escape the conclusion that donating 10 percent of one's income is not overly demanding. On the one hand, donating 10 percent will result in at most a very small decrease in one's well-being, and may even improve one's life. On the other hand, such a donation will provide enormous benefits to others, at least one hundred times as much benefit as one could provide to oneself, and plausibly much more. Donating 10 percent is much more than most people do. But morality requires at least this much.

DIFFERENT THEORIES OF WELL-BEING

So far we have relied on economists' measures of well-being. But one might question the relevance of these measures to philosophical issues; presumably such measures rely on assumptions about the nature of well-being, which might be philosophically controversial. In this section we consider two objections.

First, we have looked at two primary measures of well-being: whole life evaluations (as measured by surveys of life satisfaction) and experiential sampling. These two different metrics naturally measure two different conceptions of well-being. The whole life evaluation metric, insofar as it asks people their all-things-considered views on how their life is going, is a natural measure of well-being if one endorses a preference-satisfaction account of well-being. The experiential sampling metric, which takes the integral over time of how good one is feeling at a particular moment, seems to be a natural measure of well-being if one endorses a hedonistic account of well-being. We can make our argument perfectly well with either metric, so our argument should satisfy both preference-satisfactionists and hedonists.

Things are a little more complicated with respect to objective list theorists. Indeed it's difficult to make an argument to them directly because there are many possible items on the list of objective goods and many possible ways in which one could propose that cardinal comparisons in objective conceptions of well-being should be made between different people. But we believe that our argument should be compelling even to objective theorists.

All plausible objective theorists would consider positive conscious states as one of the objective goods.[1] And, as we have seen, experiential sampling seems to be a natural measure of positive conscious states. So even if we can't definitively say that the benefits to the extreme poor of donating 10 percent are hundreds of times as great as the costs to oneself of donating 10 percent, we can say that *with respect to one of the objective goods*, this is true.

Similarly most or all objective theories would count health as one of the objective goods. And, again, we saw that the discrepancy in health benefit that can be gained with a given amount of money varies by a factor of over 1,000, depending on whether one is trying to benefit oneself or trying to benefit the extreme poor. Given, therefore, that we have grounds for supposing there to be such a difference in impact on well-being for the two objective goods for which there are good measures available, it's reasonable to suppose that we would reach a similar conclusion if we had measures available of the other objective goods.

Perhaps one could reject our conclusion if one believed that there were certain "higher" goods—such as enjoyment of great art or engaging in philosophy—that lexically dominate the benefits we can provide for others by donating to charity and that are accessible only to those of a given income level. In that case, donating a proportion of one's income would reduce one's ability to enjoy higher goods, merely in exchange for others to enjoy lower goods. This objection, however, does not trouble us, because we do not think that a view of well-being that has such radically anti-egalitarian implications is one that anyone should endorse.

A second objection concerns *adaptive preferences,* i.e., preferences that are formed merely because of limitations on the set of available options for the agent (Bruckner 2009). One might reasonably think that the satisfaction of adaptive preferences do not make a person better off. For example, a slave may come to desire that she be enslaved because forming such a desire is the best way of dealing with a terrible situation. We could raise a similar issue with respect to hedonic states. Even if the slave finds her situation pleasant (as a result of forming a desire to be enslaved), we intuitively might wish to deny that such "adaptive experiences" make her life better.

One might worry that the phenomenon of adaptive preferences infects the empirical research we have surveyed. Once one is sufficiently rich, being able to buy fewer rather than more material goods makes very little difference to one's reported well-being. But this is, in part, because we adapt to our circumstances via rationalization and self-affirmation (Wilson and Gilbert 2005).

However, we believe that there are good reasons not to be troubled by this objection. First, failure to predict adaptation only partly explains why we overestimate the impact of income on our well-being. As well as adaptation, psychologists suggest that another part of the explanation is the *focusing illusion* (Wilson and Gilbert 2005). If someone who is not disabled is asked to consider what life would be like with a disability, his mind is immediately drawn to those aspects of life that would be negatively impacted by this condition. The particular salience of these considerations gives them a dispro-portionate place in the picture he forms of life with a disability: he forgets to take due account of the many other things that contribute to personal well-being but which are not affected by disability. We see the outcome that we are thinking about as mattering more to our happiness simply because we are focusing on it at the time.

Second, the objector must argue not only that people's preferences are adaptive, but that they are *objectionably* adaptive. For example, if your long-term partner breaks up with you, you may come to see that former partner in a different light: his flaws might become more salient; his positive characteristics might come to seem less important. This is a natural part of coping with loss, and, it seems to us, is genuinely relevant to assessing someone's well-being. All other things being equal, someone who did not have such psy-chological coping mechanisms would be made worse off by a ro-mantic breakup than someone who does have such mechanisms.

Third, as previously noted, when we look at more objective measures of well-being, such as risks of death, we get even stronger conclusions in terms of the ratio between how much we can benefit ourselves and how much we can benefit others. But such objective measures of well-being are not contaminated by adaptive preferences.

Fourth, and most important, if we are concerned with the phe-nomenon of adaptive preferences, we must be concerned with it in relation *both* to the preferences of those in rich countries and those in poor countries because our argument concerns the *ratio* between benefits that one can provide to oneself and benefits that one can pro-vide to others. If we worry that the comparatively poor in rich countries overestimate their own well-being because of adaptive preferences, we must worry to a far greater degree that the very poor overestimate their own well-being because of adaptive preferences. Indeed in the literature on adaptive preferences, it is the adaptive preferences of the indigent or oppressed that have typically been taken to be the most objectionable as part of a theory of well-being (Nussbaum 2001). This makes sense because it is the very poorest who have by far the largest constraints on the options available to them. Given this, rejecting the satisfaction of adaptive preferences as contributing to a person's well-being will only make our argument stronger.

CONCLUSION

In this chapter we considered the following principle:

Very Weak Principle of Sacrifice: Most middle-class members of affluent countries ought, morally, to use at least 10 percent of their income to effectively improve the lives of others.

We argued that, unlike Singer's two proposed principles of sacrifice, there is not even a pro tanto case that the Very Weak Principle of Sacrifice is too demanding, because this principle is not demanding at all. Following this principle would have small or no costs to one's well-being but would result in very large benefits for some of the poorest people in the world.

NOTE

1. As Parfit (1984, 4) writes, "On all theories, happiness and pleasure are at least part of what makes our lives go better for us, and misery and pain are at least part of what makes our lives go worse. These claims would be made by any plausible Objective List Theory. . . . On all theories, the Hedonistic Theory is at least part of the truth."

REFERENCES

Aknin, Lara, Michael Norton, and Elizabeth Dunn (2009). "From Wealth to Wellbeing? Money Matters, but Less Than People Think." *Journal of Positive Psychology* 4: 523–527.

Aknin, Lara et al. (2010). "Prosocial Spending and Wellbeing: Cross-Cultural Evidence for a Psychological Universal." Working Paper 11-038. Harvard Business School, Cambridge, MA.

Boyd, Norman et al. (1990). "Whose Utilities for Decision Analysis?" *Medical Decision Making* 10: 58–67.

Braithwaite, R. Scott et al. (2008). "What Does the Value of Modern Medicine Say about the $50,000 per Quality-Adjusted Life-Year Decision Rule?" *Medical Care* 46: 349–356.

Bruckner, D. (2009). "In Defense of Adaptive Preferences." *Philosophical Studies* 142: 307–324.

Charities Aid Foundation (2015). "UK Giving 2014." April. https://www.cafonline.org/docs/default-source/about-us-publications/caf-ukgiving2014.

Diener, Ed and Robert Biswas-Diener (2002). "Will Money Increase Subjective Wellbeing? A Literature Review and Guide to Needed Research." *Social Indicators Research* 57: 119–169.

Diener, Ed et al. (2010). "Wealth and Happiness across the World: Material Prosperity Predicts Life Evaluation, Whereas Psychosocial Prosperity Predicts Positive Feeling." *Journal of Personality and Social Psychology* 99: 52–61.

Dunn, Elizabeth, Lara Aknin, and Michael Norton (2008). "Spending Money on Others Promotes Happiness." *Science* 319: 1687–1688.

Dunn, Elizabeth, Daniel Gilbert, and Timothy Wilson (2011). "If Money Doesn't Make You Happy Then You Probably Aren't Spending It Right." *Journal of Consumer Psychology* 21: 115–125.

Easterlin, Richard (2001). "Income and Happiness: Towards a Unified Theory." *Economic Journal* 111: 465–484.

Food and Agriculture Organization (2015). *State of Food Insecurity in the World: Meeting the 2015 International Hunger Targets. Taking Stock of Uneven Progress*. http://www.fao.org/3/a-i4646e.pdf.

Gilbert, Daniel et al. (1998). "Immune Neglect: A Source of Durability Bias in Affective Forecasting." *Journal of Personality and Social Psychology* 75: 617–638.

GiveWell (2015). "Cost-Effectiveness Analysis of LLIN Distribution." http://www.givewell.org/files/DWDA percent202009/Interventions/GiveWell_cost-effectiveness_analysis_2015.xlsx.

Giving Institute (2017). "Giving USA 2017 Highlights: An Overview of Giving in 2016." https://store.givingusa.org/products/giving-usa-2017-report-highlights

Hooker, Brad (2009). "The Demandingness Objection." In Tim Chappell (ed.), *The Moral Problem of Demandingness: New Philosophical Essays*. New York: Palgrave, 148–162.

Kagan, Shelly (1989). *The Limits of Morality*. Oxford: Oxford University Press, 231–270.

Kahneman, Daniel (1999). "Objective Happiness." In Daniel Kahneman, Ed Diener, and Norbert Schwarz (eds.), *Wellbeing: The Foundations of Hedonic Psychology*. New York: Russell Sage, 3–25.

Kahneman, Daniel et al. (2006). "Would You Be Happier If You Were Richer? A Focusing Illusion." *Science* 312: 1908–1910.

MacAskill, William (2015). *Doing Good Better: How Effective Altruism Can Help You Help Others, Do Work that Matters, and Make Smarter Choices about Giving Back*. New York: Penguin.

National Institute for Health Care Excellence (2014). *Developing NICE Guidelines: The Manual*. https://www.nice.org.uk/article/pmg20/.

Nussbaum, Martha (2001). "Adaptive Preferences and Women's Options." *Economics and Philosophy* 17: 67–88.

Organisation for Economic Co-operation and Development (2015). "Development Aid Stable in 2014 but Flows to Poorest Countries Still Falling." http://www.oecd.org/dac/stats/development-aid-stable-in-2014-but-flows-to-poorest-countries-still-falling.htm.

Parfit, Derek (1984). *Reasons and Persons*. Oxford: Oxford University Press.

Sackett, Daniel and George Torrance (1978). "The Utility of Different Health States as Perceived by the General Public." *Journal of Chronic Diseases* 31: 697–704.

Shiffrin, Seanna (1991). "Moral Autonomy and Agent-Centred Options." *Analysis* 5: 244–254.

Singer, Peter (1972). "Famine, Affluence, and Morality." *Philosophy & Public Affairs* 31: 229–243.

Slote, Michael (1985). *Common-sense Morality and Consequentialism*. London: Routledge and Kegan Paul.

Social Security Administration (2014). "Measures of Central Tendency for Wage Data." https://www.ssa.gov/oact/cola/central.html.

Stevenson, Betsey and Justin Wolfers (2013). "Subjective Wellbeing and Income: Is There Any Evidence of Satiation?" *American Economic Review* 103: 598–604.

Stone, Arthur, Saul Shiffman, and Marten deVries (1999). "Ecological Momentary Assessment." In Daniel Kahneman, Ed Diener, and Norbert Schwarz (eds.), *Wellbeing: The Foundations of Hedonic Psychology*. New York: Russell Sage, 26–39.

Tengs, Tammy O. et al. (1995). "Five-Hundred Life-Saving Interventions and Their Cost-Effectiveness." *Risk Analysis* 15: 369–390.

UNdata (2015). "Somalia." http://data.un.org/CountryProfile.aspx?crName=somalia.

UNICEF (2015). "Levels and Trends in Child Mortality Report 2015: Estimates Developed by the UN Inter-agency Group for Child Mortality Estimation."

http://www.who.int/maternal_child_adolescent/documents/levels_trends_child_mortality_2015/en/.

UNESCO (2014). "Adult and Youth Literacy." *UIS Fact Sheet* 29. http://unesdoc.unesco.org/images/0022/002295/229504e.pdf.

UNESCO (2015). *Education for All 2000–2015: Achievements and Challenges.* Paris: United Nations Educational, Scientific and Cultural Organization.

Williams, Bernard (1973). "A Critique of Utilitarianism." In J. J. C. Smart and Bernard Williams, *Utilitarianism: For and Against.* Cambridge, UK: Cambridge University Press, 77–150.

Wilson, Timothy and Daniel Gilbert (2005). "Affective Forecasting: Knowing What to Want." *Current Directions in Psychological Science* 14, 131–134.

World Bank (2015). "World Policy Research Note No. 3: Ending Extreme Poverty and Sharing Prosperity. Progress and Policies." http://www.worldbank.org/en/research/brief/policy-research-note-03-ending-extreme-poverty-and-sharing-prosperity-progress-and-policies.

World Health Organization and UNICEF (2015). *Progress on Sanitation and Drinking Water: 2015 Update and MDG Assessment.* New York: UNICEF.

World Value Survey Group (1994). *World Values Survey, 1981–1984 and 1990–1993.* Ann Arbor, MI: Institute for Social Research, ICPSR.

Chapter 7

Afterword

Justice and Charitable Giving

PAUL WOODRUFF

We have ethical reasons for charitable giving that are not philanthropic. Justice, for example, provides a number of reasons for giving that count against philanthropy in some cases. Philanthropic reasoning may direct you to do the most good that you can with your resources, but justice may flash a yellow or even a red light against such philanthropy. So we cannot explore the ethics of philanthropy fully without considering the ways in which justice bears on charitable giving. What follows is an overview of considerations that bear on charitable giving and belong to justice broadly construed. My aim in this chapter is to show that reasoning based on justice has a place in decisions about charitable giving. We must not consider philanthropic reasons alone; we must also consider what justice calls on us to do. In some cases justice trumps philanthropy. Ethics is complicated; no one sort of reasoning suits every case.

JUSTICE THROUGH RESTITUTION

> Having the resources to practice such beneficence as depends on
> the goods of fortune is, for the most part, a result of certain human
> beings being favored through the injustice of the government,
> which introduces an inequality of wealth that makes others need
> their beneficence. Under such circumstances, does a rich man's help
> to the needy, on which he so readily prides himself as something
> meritorious, really deserve to be called beneficence at all? (Kant
> [1797] 1996, [6:454] 203)[1]

So Kant, in the *Metaphysics of Morals*. His larger theory gives him a
tool for distinguishing two kinds of charitable giving. On the one
hand, the duty of beneficence is a wide (or imperfect) duty. By "beneficence" he means what we mean by philanthropic action. We
must do something by way of philanthropy, but we are permitted to
carry out our philanthropic duties in a variety of ways, choosing how
much to give and to whom, as Hill points out in this volume. On the
other hand, our duty to restore goods unjustly taken would have to
be narrow (or perfect). A thief must return the thing stolen, or at
least the value of the thing stolen, to its rightful owners. This duty
of restitution is perfect in Kant's terms: it clearly directs how much
and to whom the return must be made. As the theft was wrong to
begin with, we may well question whether any moral worth attaches
to making restitution. Restitution is not beneficent and it is not philanthropic; it is a discharge of debts.

Kant appears to be right about this. Elizabeth Ashford argues
convincingly in this volume that first-world wealth was derived
from exploiting the third world, and that, therefore, the first world
has a debt to pay to the third. A similar injustice may be found inside
a first-world country: if the great wealth of a family has been derived

from exploiting workers or consumers, then that family owes a debt to those exploited or their descendants.

I do not claim to know a general way to determine when such charges of exploitation are true, or, if they are found to be true, what restitution is required. But clearly the restitution argument applies to all exploitation, both local and foreign. In general any unjust economic structure can give rise to claims for restitution. By an unjust structure I mean any arrangement in which some people are permitted to accumulate wealth at the expense of others. Those who have profited from unjust structures have no right to their wealth. If they return it to those who have been deprived, they are in effect returning stolen goods to their owners.

This argument is not specific to thievery or other forms of injustice. If I pick up lost property from the street, or in any other way find someone else's property in my hands, I have a duty to return it. You would be to blame if you kept the wallet you found in the back seat of the cab. In general you do not have to be guilty of any wrongdoing in order to have a duty to restore property to its owners.

If you are guilty of wrongdoing, however, you may owe more than restitution. You may need to give up more than you have taken by way of atoning for the wrongs you have done. In other words, you may have a duty to go beyond restitution to *reparation*—beyond a return of stolen goods to the need to compensate victims for acts of violence or injustice. For example, many people hold that institutions and families are not entitled to wealth they have inherited from ancestors who wrung it out of the labor of people who were enslaved. That labor was stolen by violence against those enslaved, and for this theft restitution is due. And beyond that, something is due to atone for the violence and injustice by which the labor was stolen. Such families owe reparations to the enslaved people or their descendants. Other cases may be less obvious, but the principle is clear. Those who extorted wealth by violence are not only not entitled to that wealth; they must also make reparations to those from whom it was extorted.[2]

In what follows I will argue that we have a number of duties of justice besides those of making restitution or reparation. All such duties of justice are narrow to some degree. This distinguishes them from philanthropy. Our thief might do more good by giving the stolen goods to Oxfam than by returning them to their owners. But the owners would be right to insist that the stolen goods be returned to them. Such duties of justice (unlike the general duty of philanthropy) must fall outside the scope of act utilitarianism. We are not right to act for the best outcome when justice demands otherwise.

Kant's distinction is helpful in this way: philanthropic duty is wide or imperfect, while duties of justice are narrow or perfect to some extent.[3] You may carry out your philanthropic duty in many different ways; for example, you may freely choose your beneficiaries, so long as they are in need, and, whatever choices you make, you remain philanthropic. But your duties of making restitution are particular: your beneficiaries must be among those who lost wealth as a result of your accumulation. If you give elsewhere you fail in justice, even if you do more good.

Acts of philanthropy and justice differ in what Kant calls perfection; they also differ in moral worth. Philanthropy is meritorious in itself, but there is no special merit in declining to profit from injustice—only a loss of merit for those who consent to profit from injustice. We do not praise the nonthief for not being a thief. Should we praise thieves for returning stolen goods after a change of heart? The change of heart is good, but the goods must be returned whether or not the thief's heart has changed.

In some cases we have reason to blame people even when they return wealth to which they have no right. Suppose I an investing your pension on your behalf and I line my own pockets from your funds by collecting excessive fees. If I then return part or even all of what I have taken, I am still a thief. And my act of returning money to your pension is not meritorious. The act will even be blameworthy—the reverse of meritorious—if I claim merit for, and feel smug about, returning the stolen goods, especially if I appeal to that return in an attempt to justify my habit of stealing. So the wealthy in unjust societies may actually make themselves more blameworthy, not by making restitution as such but by the *attitudes* with which they make restitution for the injustice behind their accumulations of wealth.

STRUCTURAL INJUSTICE

There are two ways in which charitable giving can protect structural injustice. The first, mentioned earlier, is by giving donors a smug feeling that helps them deceive themselves about the injustice they exploit. "Look how generous we are!" they say to themselves, while continuing to extract wealth unjustly from others. Suppose I, the pension thief, make gifts to my clients out of my ill-gotten gains, while continuing to collect fees that are not justified. My giving salves my conscience, and may even make my clients feel that I have treated them well. In such a case, my giving masks and protects a continuing injustice.[4]

The second way, the main subject of this section, applies to donors who are truly good-hearted but whose giving tends to disguise the need for structural change. In that case, charitable giving may allow structural injustice to continue by hiding its symptoms. Charitable giving, in a structurally unjust society, may be thought to compound injustice by perpetuating it. You may save people from starving by giving them handouts (thereby allowing the unjust system to look relatively humane), but you may serve justice better if you do nothing to shore up an unjust regime in this way, while using your resources to promote a more just structure.

If I give $100 to an agency that feeds starving people, I may save a number of lives and dampen the anger that would otherwise lead to revolution. If so, I am inadvertently helping unjust rulers to preserve the conditions that are leading to starvation. Your handouts could keep people from feeling the pain that might lead to a just revolution. On the other hand, I could give the same sum to Amnesty International or some other agency that promotes justice, and this might do more good in the long run. In the same way, a medical team may treat a patient's symptoms so well that the patient does not seek a cure from the disease, with the result that the patient will die sooner than necessary.

Relieving symptoms may not do the most good. An accurate calculation of costs and benefits might lead a utilitarian to the same conclusion as the argument based on justice—if it finds that the short-term benefits of giving in such a case are overshadowed by the long-term costs. But the advocate of justice can still argue that, regardless of such calculations, we should never act to shore up injustice. Justice, as a reason, is opposed to philanthropy in such cases.[5] We don't have to agree with the extreme motto, *Fiat justitia, pereat mundus,* "Let justice be done even if it destroys the world." We may nevertheless prefer a just order to a more prosperous one, if the more prosperous outcome is not more just.

FAIR SHARE: PAYING FOR BENEFITS

For almost any mortgage that I might have, I would do more good by sending payments to Oxfam than to the bank to which I am in debt. And yet it is to the bank that my payments are owed, in accordance with justice. In addition to such formal debts, we all have informal debts of various kinds, and these must be considered as we make ethical decisions about charitable giving.

Suppose you benefited from a Princeton education for which you did not have to pay the full cost. A large part of the cost of your education was carried by donated funds and the income from a donated endowment. This was good luck for you. At the time of your education you could not have afforded the full cost, but now you have become wealthy and can afford to donate substantially to your old university. Do you (as an ethical matter) owe Princeton as much as you can now afford to pay toward the cost, looking back? Or does justice require that you donate as much as you can afford, looking forward, so that as many younger people as possible can benefit as you did? Or, if Princeton is so rich that it does not need your donation, do you have a duty to donate to another school, whose needs are greater? If these questions remain open, as it appears they must, then the duty to pay your fair share for education is not perfectly narrow. But it is not wide either: this duty is narrowly to education, as it is for your *education* that you are indebted.[6] You won't pay this debt by giving money to an agency that fights malaria—even though, by doing so, you would be carrying out your philanthropic duty.

In a developed culture such as ours, most of us enjoy benefits for which we are not required to pay the full cost. The price of admission to an art museum barely scratches the surface of the cost of keeping the museum's doors open. The ticket I buy for a chamber music concert may cover less than half of my share of the cost of the concert; the remainder is picked up by donors. Am I, in return for benefits received, under an obligation to pick up a share of the expense of those benefits, if I can afford to do so?

Rawls (1971, 343) has clearly stated the principle that covers such fair share arguments: "We are not to gain from the cooperative efforts of others without doing our fair share."[7] Such civic amenities are made available to members of the community at a low cost in order that they may be widely enjoyed. If you willingly take regular advantage of the amenities, then you have a moral obligation to pick up your fair share of the tab, or else you will be a freeloader. What is your fair share? That would have to be a function of the resources available after you have met your needs and your more pressing obligations. Perhaps your philanthropic duties to prevent starvation and disease in the third world are so great that you do not have enough left to give to museums or concerts. Very well. But the fair share argument given here must have some weight in your calculation. Effective altruism may trump your obligations to donate to the arts and education that you have enjoyed, but these obligations are real nonetheless and must be weighed along with other duties.

You may avoid such obligations, however, as you have the choice to forgo enjoying the arts, and you may also decide to educate yourself at no expense to donors. But there are some benefits you cannot forgo in any organized community. An opportunity is a benefit whether or not you use it to the full; if there are parks in your town you have the opportunity to enjoy them, so even if you do not choose to take that opportunity you owe something for their upkeep. This obligation is recognized in your local tax bill.

Then there are the safety nets provided by local nonprofit organizations—the food bank that would feed your family if they were suddenly impoverished, for example. You may never need it, but it is there for you if you do, and perhaps someone close to you, unbeknownst to you, is depending on it. Having a safety net is a benefit, and you owe your fair share for keeping it up, no matter what chances you have of falling into it. That principle is recognized in the purchase of insurance. If your house does not burn down, your fire insurance is still worth the cost.

Robert Nozick (1974, 93–94) has made an objection to fair share arguments: Even if you have enjoyed the benefits of a certain service and even if you cannot turn off those benefits (his example is a broadcasting system), you are not obligated to do your share to keep the benefits coming. You have the right to spend your resources in ways you choose, especially if the cost to you of your fair share is greater than the benefit to you of the service. Free-riders in the world of philanthropy are not like subway passengers who choose to travel without buying a ticket and get away with it. Of those who decline to take part in a philanthropy scheme, he writes, "They don't desire to be free riders; they don't care about the ride at all" (267). This objection has no force against the reciprocity argument when it is based on practices one has voluntarily joined, such as I describe below in the case of the U.S. marines. Joining such practices is like boarding the subway. But Nozick's objection shows that we must take Rawls's claim weakly. I prefer to state it this way: You have reasons to pay your fair share for benefits you receive, but those reasons may not prevail in every case over other considerations.

Most of our fair share obligations are local, with the result that many small philanthropists are vividly aware of their local obligations. That may explain why a large percentage of charitable donations is given to local causes.[8] If I am right, these donations are not philanthropic in the strict sense; they are fair share donations that discharge an obligation of justice. Unlike most obligations of justice, however, fair share obligations are not entirely narrow. The concert-goer, for example, can decide which concerts to support and to what degree. College graduates do not have a duty that prescribes exactly how much they should give or to whom. All that is clear is that they should give something to education in return for what they have received. Philanthropic duties such as effective altruism compete with fair share obligations, but it is not obvious that effective altruism trumps the fair share argument in every case.

FAIR SHARE: RECIPROCITY AND RESCUE

Beyond your duty to support the safety nets that protect you stands a more active duty: the duty to rescue one in need. Both duties can be understood as belonging to the more general duty of mutual aid, which (in my view) falls under justice broadly construed, although Rawls assigns this to the category of natural duty rather than justice. He explains the value of this principle as follows:

> A sufficient ground for adopting this duty is its pervasive effect on the quality of everyday life. The public knowledge that we are living in a society in which we can depend on others to come to our assistance in difficult circumstances is itself of great value.... The primary value of the principle is not measured by the help we actually receive but rather by the sense of confidence and trust in other men's good intentions and the knowledge that they are there if we need them. (1971, 339; 1999, 298)

The last phrase is important for us: "the knowledge that they are there if we need them." That seems to make the duty of mutual aid primarily local, because, as a practical matter, we can know that others are there to help only within a specific range or community. (In the next section I will discuss how this duty might be given a scope beyond the local.) When you rescue someone who might, on another occasion, rescue you, you may think of yourself as rendering mutual aid. But you cannot think this when, by writing a check, you rescue someone unknown to you, far away in an impoverished country; in that case you do not need to imagine the rescued person ever being in a position to rescue you (although you may be rich enough in imagination to do so). Whatever duty moves you in the distant case you most likely understand as philanthropic, rather than mutual.

The duty of mutual aid, however, is generally local and often connected to specific practices or professions. Mariners have a duty to rescue other mariners in distress. This duty has deep roots in the practices of the sea and is narrow in the following sense: the mariners you must rescue are precisely the ones you can safely reach. If you see a distress signal, you must alter course toward the troubled craft, unless that would lead to your own shipwreck. The mariners in distress would do the same for you. You would be a freeloader if you enjoyed the security of this practice without doing your share of rescue work.[9]

Young people training for the U.S. Marines are taught that they have a duty to rescue any other marine even at risk of their lives. Marine veterans have told me that they believed, with good reason, that other marines truly would lay down their lives for them. Knowing that gave them confidence in undertaking dangerous missions. To join the U.S. Marines with a determination to let other people do the rescuing would be freeloading. When military people who have performed dangerous rescues are asked why they took such risks, they often answer, "Because they would have done the same for me."

Note that for rescue cases in the U.S. Marines, the duty is stronger than the one given by Singer's (1972) strong principle.[10] If you sign on as a U.S. Marine, you have a duty to risk your life in rescuing a fellow U.S. Marine, even if the expected outcome is not the best. Imagine a situation in which a calculation of cost and benefit shows that it is better not to rescue a wounded U.S. Marine, better for all overall if you leave her for the ferocious enemy to torture and kill. The duty of rescue is still incumbent on the other U.S. Marines in such a case, regardless of the cost—because they know that she would join the effort to rescue them if they were in her place. Similarly strong principles may apply to people whose jobs entail rescuing others, such as firefighters. But these are not based on mutual aid, as are the duties for mariners and U.S. Marines.

Underlying all practices of mutual aid is a larger principle related to justice: reciprocity.

> Reciprocity: If I voluntarily engage in a certain practice and am protected by that practice, then I have an obligation to provide similar protections to others engaged in that practice.

It would seem that your duty of rescue is limited under reciprocity to those who might rescue you. Nevertheless habits developed under reciprocity can benefit those outside the practice. After their defeat at the Yalu River in Korea, marines saved each other, as they were trained to do, at risk of their lives. But they also saved army personnel who had not been trained to take such risks and probably would not have acted to save the marines.

We may have many reasons for rescuing a person in distress. Practice-based reciprocity is not the only principle that applies to such cases. The principle of reciprocity does not exclude Kantian, virtue-ethical, or utilitarian reasons for rescuing, but it is more powerful when based on certain specific practices than it is under any general ethical theory. Its power depends on its being partial in a way that ethical theory usually is not.

Philanthropic reasons are weaker than those of reciprocity. Even landlubbers can fulfill a duty of philanthropy by contributing to a rescue fund for sailors, and the duty is the same no matter how far away the sailors may be. But there is little risk in writing checks. Sailors too may donate to a philanthropic fund for distressed mariners, but they have an additional duty, and a stronger one, based on the practices of the sea. The duty they have toward each other under reciprocity is specific to sailors in distress within their reach, in view of the specific practice from which all sailors benefit. Another difference: duties of rescue tied to specific practices are usually more demanding than general philanthropic ones: you may have a duty to give your life for another.

The training of U.S. Marines and the practices of sailors seem to help people develop attitudes toward rescue that go beyond reciprocity. We may find that former U.S. Marines or retired sailors are more likely to be good Samaritans than others. If so, they are better people for not being limited by a practice of reciprocity or even by the more general principle of mutual aid. "Because they are U.S. Marines and would do the same for me" can grow into "Because they are fellow human beings, and human beings are moved by nature to assist one another." Rawls may have had this in the back of his mind when he called mutual aid a duty of nature. This thought carries us beyond practices and even beyond the confines of community. We need not believe in the possibility of mutual aid as a universal practice, so long as we believe that all human beings are born to be mutual aiders.

BEYOND PRACTICES OF RECIPROCITY

The duty of rescue can be understood in several ways. A child who has fallen into a well calls for rescue, and most people feel that any passersby ought to rescue the child if they can complete the rescue without undue risk or cost.[11] Where does this "ought" come from? A moral theory would be defective if it did not provide good reasons for the duty of rescue in a case that does not involve reciprocity (at least not obviously). Singer uses the child example to support his strong principle. His argument appears to be mainly utilitarian.[12]

Intuitionists have no trouble summoning intuitions in favor of rescue in such circumstances. Mencius used the child in the well example as a thought experiment to show that any normal human being is born with at least the beginnings of the virtue of benevolence, which reveals itself in us when we suppose that, as passersby, we would feel that we ought to rescue the child; in acknowledging this feeling we "give away" the presence in us of a heart that we might have been hiding before (Ivanhoe 2000, 19).

No matter how good our reasons are for rescuing the child in the well as we pass by, they intuitively seem weaker when applied to the rescue of hundreds of thousands of children on the other side of the globe. This is a puzzle. What difference should large numbers make? Or great distances? Technology has conquered distance. We can now come virtually face to face with faraway suffering, and we can pool our funds in order to rescue large numbers. If we can achieve a greater good by ignoring one nearby child in order to rescue dozens of distant ones, perhaps we should do so. If the distant ones are far less expensive to save, then we will do more good by ignoring the near one and sending help to those far away.

Most ethical theories hold that reasons in ethics should be impartial. Kantians and utilitarians would agree. Partiality to nearby children in nearby wells, as opposed to distant children in distant wells, would (on such theories) be irrational and wrong. Yet most charitable giving is affected by partiality for the local. Are local donors irrational in this?

We have seen that fair share arguments offer some rational support for local giving, while the argument for making restitution supports giving to peoples who have been exploited on our behalf, whether they are near or distant. I now want to explore the possibility that the principle of reciprocity can be extended to all human beings and even beyond them, to other sentient creatures capable of empathy.

Mencius appears to be correct in thinking that human beings are born with a capacity for something like empathy, as the child-in-the-well example is supposed to show. If he is right, then I can reasonably expect that faraway people from quite different cultures would rescue a grandchild of mine if the need arose. Unlikely, but not inconceivable. With this in mind, I could well conceive of my international rescue efforts in terms of reciprocity. This reciprocity would not be based on a specific practice, such as that of mariners or the U.S. Marines, but instead on our common humanity—on our exercise of what it is to be human.[13]

NOTES

1. Kant ([1797] 1996, [6.453] 202) distinguishes benevolence from beneficence. "Benevolence is satisfaction in the happiness of others"; this "costs us nothing," whereas *beneficence*, which is a duty, requires action. It is "to promote according to one's means the happiness of others without hoping for something in return."
2. Consider the example of Georgetown University recognizing this duty (Swarns 2016).
3. See Kant's ([1797] 1996, [6.390] 153–154) distinction between wide and narrow duties, which is roughly the same as his distinction between imperfect duties and perfect ones. Philosophers have differed over how to understand this. In this chapter I treat perfection as a matter of degree. The duty to restore stolen goods is perfect in that the thief's duty is specific as to both the amount owed and the people to whom it is owed. But the duty to make up for structural injustice, occurring over many years, is mixed. It may be clear to whom the debt is owed—to those who were exploited or their heirs—but not clear how large the debt is.

4. In some cases giving may actually constitute an injustice, as it does when it raises the donor's self-esteem at the cost of the recipient's.

5. On this issue, see Ashford's careful argument in this volume.

6. Boesch, in this volume, follows St. Thomas Aquinas in taking this to be a debt not of justice but of piety.

7. I am treating fair share arguments as falling under justice. Rawls (1999, 98, 297–298) does not do so; his duty of mutual aid is a duty of nature, and not (in his terms) an obligation. See Nozick's (1974, 93–94) objection to Rawls.

8. On local giving see Singer 2010, 15–16. On total giving, see MacAskill et al., this volume. For a strong argument on behalf of effective altruism, see MacAskill 2015.

9. Would you be a freeloader if you held back from the duty of rescue because you were determined never to accept help from another sailor? I think you would; by going to see you accept the age-old practices of the sea.

10. Singer's (1972) strong principle: "The strong version, which required us to prevent bad things from happening unless in doing so we would be sacrificing something of comparable moral significance, does seem to require reducing ourselves to the level of marginal utility. I should also say that the strong version seems to me to be the correct one. I proposed the more moderate version—that we should prevent bad occurrences unless, to do so, we had to sacrifice something morally significant—only in order to show that, even on this surely undeniable principle, a great change in our way of life is required. On the more moderate principle, it may not follow that we ought to reduce ourselves to the level of marginal utility, for one might hold that to reduce oneself and one's family to this level is to cause something significantly bad to happen. Whether this is so I shall not discuss, since, as I have said, I can see no good reason for holding the moderate version of the principle rather than the strong version." I am suggesting that reciprocity might call on us to sacrifice something of greater—not merely equal—moral significance.

11. Much hangs on what we mean by "without undue risk or cost" here. In Singer's (1972) moderate proposal it means "without sacrificing something morally significant."

12. See Singer (1972; 2010, 3) for his take on the drowning child. His "basic argument" (2010, 15–16) leads to the conclusion that it is wrong not to give aid. Act utilitarians generally hold that it is wrong not to choose the action available to you that promises the best expected outcome. The effective altruism movement does not explicitly ally itself with utilitarianism but relies on moral intuitions about such cases. See Singer (2010, 4); his effective altruism allows for a variety of values (2015, 8–9). MacAskill (2015, 31–32), however, does explicitly appeal to consequentialist reasoning.

13. For further reading on this topic, see especially Salamon (2003) and Lichtenberg (2014). Also see the essays in Ilingworth, et al (2011) and Zinsmeister (2016).

REFERENCES

Illingworth, Patricia, Thomas Pogge, and Leif Wenar (2011). *Giving Well: The Ethics of Philanthropy*. New York: Oxford University Press.

Ivanhoe, P. (2000). *Confucian Self-Cultivation*. 2d edition. Indianapolis, IN: Hackett.

Kant, I. ([1797] 1996). *The Metaphysics of Morals*. Edited by Mary Gregor. Cambridge, UK: Cambridge Texts in the History of Philosophy.

Lichtenberg, Judith (2014). *Distant Strangers: Ethics, Psychology, and Global Poverty*. Cambridge, UK: Cambridge University Press.

MacAskill, W. (2015). *Doing Good Better: How Effective Altruism Can help You Make a Difference*. New York: Gotham Books.

Nozick, Robert (1974). *Anarchy, State, and Utopia*. New York: Basic Books.

Rawls, John (1971). *A Theory of Justice*. Cambridge, MA: Harvard University Press.

Rawls, John (1999). *A Theory of Justice*. 2d edition. Cambridge, MA: Harvard University Press.

Salamon, Julie (2003). *Rambam's Ladder: A Meditation on Generosity and Why It Is Necessary to Give*. New York: Workman.

Singer, Peter (1972). "Famine, Affluence, and Morality." *Philosophy and Public Affairs* 1 (1), https://www.utilitarian.net/singer/by/1972.

Singer, Peter (2010). *The Life You Can Save*. New York: Random House.

Singer, Peter (2015). *The Most Good You Can Do: How Effective Altruism Is Changing Ideas about Living Ethically*. New Haven, CT: Yale University Press.

Swarns, Rachel L. (2016). "Georgetown University Plans Steps to Atone for Slave Past." *New York Times*, September 1. http://www.nytimes.com/2016/09/02/us/slaves-georgetown-university.html?_r=0.

Zinsmeister, Karl (2016). *What Comes Next? How Private Givers Can Rescue America in an Era of Political Frustration*. Washington, DC: Philanthropy Roundtable.

INDEX